NOTHING'S SO BAD THAT IT COULDN'T BE WORSE

~~*Raymond Poole*~~

Published by The Book Hub Publishing Group

For further information re national & international distribution

www.bookhubpublishing.com info@bookhubpublishing.com

@BookHubPublish

First Edition 2020

ISBN 978-1-9160883-3-7

A catalogue record for this book is available from the British Library.

PROLOGUE

To coin an old phrase, life is a journey but, more importantly, as we progress along that journey we gather attributes to our self-being that help carry us through inevitable events that we will encounter. No two people have the same journey whether in their personal or business life. Norms are not the norms when it comes to our make-up as, like snowflakes, each of us is unique. We are the outcome of that journey, those destinations and the intermittent stops we make along the way.

The genesis for this book was centred on my encounter with cancer, however for the reader to comprehend how I approached that particular stop in my life they would first have to understand my journey to date. Albeit, cancer was one particular 'stop,' it acts as the conduit to this book, but it is not the full story and I take you on a more complete journey to some of those other encounters that happened along the way. I hope you find something within that may help you on your own journey. Have a great life as it is a one way ticket. And the train never runs to our schedule.

DEDICATION

This book is dedicated to the young girl I first met aged 10 and grew into the young teenager who whilst wearing her orange Gucci t-shirt, faded denim jeans and flip-flops said yes to me when on 01-JUN-1978 I asked her to be my girlfriend. We were then aged fifteen years old and have been together since. She is my strength and my weakness all wrapped in one, her courage and commitment to me has been a steadfast constant in my life. With her I am a better person, and because of her I am whom I have become. She is the strength that holds our love constant.

It is also dedicated to my six year old self. I am sorry I was not stronger when you needed me to be, I am sorry it has taken fifty years to publicly admit your pain and torment. You deserved better and for that I will always be seeking your forgiveness.

Finally, it is dedicated to all those children whom through no fault of their own find themselves in the middle of conflict, natural disasters or a victim of the geographic territory they were born into. My heart is with you, fight long, fight strong and never give up as you are our future. We depend on your survival to show us the wrong doings of our ways. While you cry from hunger we discard our surplus food. While you cry from the cold with no shelter, we complain about the weather. As you struggle to be educated we bemoan the education system. Whilst you try to suckle from your dead mother's breast, we debate the right to breastfeed in public.

I have heard your cries and this book, above all else, is for you. May it bring you light in the darkness, shelter from the cold and food when you thought no one heard your cries. Your life is precious, it deserves to be saved and fought for. My ammunition is no more than a quiver of 26 arrows but they are aimed skilfully at the hearts that may read this book to ensure you grow to adulthood.

There is nothing more pure or innocent than a child, and it is for that reason all profits made from the sale of this book will go to UNICEF Ireland. On their behalf I thank you for purchasing it and rest assured by doing so you have made a contribution to saving a child's life.

ACKNOWLEDGEMENTS

I would like to thank the following who provided their services on pro bono basis: Karl Smyth, an award-winning graphic designer, for the cover design.

Peter McVeigh for recording some of the poetry from this book. But, more importantly, giving me the music that healed my mind. His music is the soundtrack to my life.

Guys, thanks for just being there providing an ear when required, never judging and always sympathetic.

A word of thanks to my editorial team at Book Hub Publishing; Niall, Anna and Susan.

My mother who still inspires me even though she passed away in 2014, love you mum. Finally, my father who had his own journey with colon cancer in 2007 and now in 2019 once again is fighting a return battle with cancer in his kidney, bladder and hip. Cancer, the visitor who comes for a weekend and never leaves.

CONTENTS

SOUNDTRACK TO BOOK

I want to introduce a concept with my book and that is a dedicated soundtrack. My life would be nothing without music as it is my therapist that has healed my mind on so many occasions and on different journeys throughout my life. You can listen to these tracks whilst reading the book but if you find that too distracting you can listen to them after you have put the book down. Regardless of how you listen, I hope it will bring something new to your experience of reading a book. Enjoy.

Thank you to Gareth O'Callaghan for putting the tunes in some order for me.

The playlist can be found on Spotify at

https://open.spotify.com/playlist/5eD6hVJ7JexnuwtyNoqKEf

PREFACE

This book is about my personal journey in life to date with a stop off when I disembarked to tackle cancer. My story is only complete when all the components in my life are considered as a collective unit rather than by examining any one of them in isolation. Like all of you reading this book, we've had events that have helped us become who we are today. That journey is not yet complete so there are more encounters to occur as I travel down the tracks of life. My hope is that by reading this book you will gain some comfort in knowing that you are stronger, more resilient than you think and capable of aspiring to greatness in your life.

I am not selling this book as a concept that will make you wealthy beyond your beliefs or fix any issues you may have. But rather I hope that the wealth you will gain from reading it will be that of mental health/strength and the self-confidence to know you have this, whatever "this" may be that life will throw at you. It is not a medical book, as I am not a doctor. It is simply a book written from the heart with nothing held back in order to strip naked the realities of real life and in doing so exposing my vulnerability. There are many articles, websites, books, etc. that can explain in detail all the medical information you may require to know if you, or one of your loved ones, have been recently diagnosed with cancer, a mental illness or any other life changing/threatening illness.

This is not the intention of this book. This book's theme views being inside the head of an individual struggling at times with their thoughts, fears, anxieties, frustrations and feelings they encounter on their life's journey. It is a brutally honest book with few filters applied. There will be talk about the mental impact cancer has had on me and my relationship with my wife and, indeed, life. It is a book that may act as a catalyst to start those awkward conversations you need to have if you are struggling. But before we get to that stop on my journey, we first must look at my expedition, to date, to understand why I behaved the way I did when I encountered cancer on the tracks of my own journey.

I would like to just state that I am not proclaiming to be any type of expert or indeed a model patient as I am far from either. I still have many demons to eradicate from my head and get my life back to some semblance of what it was prior to surgery. However, I can say that it is a journey I will never forget. All that said, cancer has brought many positives into my life, not least the tremendous people I have met and some I can now call friends. Our paths would never have crossed but for the cancer and, in some strange way, for that I am grateful. I hope this book proves to be of some value to others out there and indeed their loved ones so they can understand at some level what is going on inside one's head.

The Japanese have a lovely tradition called Kintsugi, literally translated it means golden ("kin") and repair ("tsugi"). This tradition uses precious metals such as liquid gold or silver to bind together the broken pieces of ceramics whilst at the same time enhancing and celebrating the cracks.

Leonard Cohen, in his beautiful song, 'Anthem' also sings about celebrating the cracks in life and how it allows the light to get in.

At some level, we all have cracks within us but just because we do, does not mean we should be discarded on a heap of redundant and broken objects. Beauty is not about external appearances but rather that thread that holds the internal fabric of your very existence; it is what goes on within and is never simple.

The way I looked at the challenges in my life is that they are merely a thread in the fabric that makes me who I am but they do not define me. I'm a product of my life experiences good and bad but I'm in control to decide if they are positive or negative.

Please note that every person's journey with any illness or obstacle in their life is different but there are similarities. Hopefully, I have captured enough to make your voyage that bit easier.

Have a safe journey and may you discover many strengths about yourself that perhaps you were not aware of before. My thoughts and best wishes are with you, especially your loved ones.

Brief encounters may only last for a moment but may impact our lives for a lifetime. Don't be blinded to the enduring impression they may have on you.

CHAPTER 1
THE FORMATIVE YEARS

Ireland's national broadcaster's first television station, Teilifis Éireann, held its inaugural broadcast on New Year's Eve 1961. Almost a year later on Christmas Eve 1962, Dublin was covered in a white blanket in preparation for the annual visit of the elusive rather large white bearded man. As dusk descended upon the city, snow fell from the grey skies gently caressing the suburbs like a sprinkling of icing sugar across a winter landscape scene on a cake. The street lights were the super troupers of this angelic dance show as the white snowflakes performed their Bolero routine intertwining and majestically bowing out as they silently left the stage to rest gently on the surfaces below.

The eerie silence that can only be found on such a night slowly crept across the city and through the many suburbs, and gradually the roads became the feathered duvet of the cars tucking them in as they remained parked outside homes immobile to venture beyond.

However, one car was making its way through the snow, slowly and steadily with a young pregnant mother sitting in the passenger seat. She was not due for at least another 6 weeks, there were anxious voices chatting in the car but trying desperately to hide their concern as she once again ignored the advice of the medical profession and decided for the second time to become pregnant. She told her mother she was just popping out to get some last minute items for Christmas morning so as not to alarm her. She was accompanied by her husband and brother-in-law. They made their way across a deserted city to the outer limits of what then seemed like civilisation to Mount Carmel hospital in Rathfarnham, Dublin. How appropriate was this scene for the night that was in it. Mary, a pregnant lady seeking refuge and help in a welcoming hostel, however this time the light that shone brightly above was that of an electric lamppost as even that night the moon was tucked away out of sight.

On arrival, she was ushered to a room and soon after her family doctor was called. He was a gentle soul who took extremely good care of Mary as he knew she was living life her way, defying all the medical advice she had been given early on in life. He had a thick Scottish accent and was of Jewish decent.

"Mary, you're a sneaky one" he said.

"I know Doctor, I am sorry for taking you away from your family on Christmas Eve."

"That's fine Mary, I am here now and let's look after you" he kindly replied.

I came screaming into this world unapologetic, the way I dare say I will leave it, unexpectedly and not in line with anyone else's timeline but my own. Later in life, my mum told me that when I was born she could hear the nuns singing carols in the hospital and it sounded like the angels where present for my birth. I often wondered how those nuns would have felt if they had known they were welcoming an atheist into the world. One born on Christmas Day! Somewhere there is an irony in that situation, a catholic woman giving birth on Christmas morning to an atheist son delivered by a Jewish doctor.

Her doctor came back up to visit her later that day, and holding me in his arms he strolled over to the window.

> "He looks a wee bit jaundice Mary. I think he may have scarlet fever but nothing to worry yourself about. He will be fine."

Here I was my first moments in this life already causing concern and making my mark to announce I have arrived.

As the debate rages on between nature versus nurture I am one of those who is of the opinion that we evolve from our surroundings and the encounters we experience in life. Therefore, I would argue you cannot really dismiss the influence of one over the other, both nature and nurture have an impact on us and who we, ultimately, become.

Like any stereotypical 1960s Irish family "the mammy" was the central force in my upbringing. Working mothers were a rarity and, in fact, the law stated at the time that if a woman was working as a civil servant upon marriage she had to resign. It's hard to believe that scenario only ended in 1973. Therefore, although this book is about my journey it would be absent of me not to mention my mum and the deep influence she had on my evolution.

My mum was a woman like no other, a force to be reckoned with but a gentle soul too. She lived for her children and all her milestones in life were based around major events in our lives such as attending school, first communion, confirmation, etc. My father was advised not to marry her as she had ill health and was not expected to live long, but he ignored that advice. She was then told not to have children as her body would not be capable of managing a pregnancy. Well, I guess you figured that one out, she ignored that advice. On giving birth to my brother in June 1960 she was warned that to have another child would definitely be terminal to her health. She had haemorrhaged a lot of blood during his birth and her lung was not capable of taking the stress of another pregnancy.

However, no one gave her that roadmap, in her mind it was unfair to have a single child, so on she went and became pregnant with me giving birth on 25th December 1962.

There were no rules that governed my mother, she defied all predictions of her demise and set her own agenda to life. She was a woman of strong faith but never blinded by the veil of deceit from the thunderous pounding of the self-righteous pulpit. Religion, to her, was not about whether you attended a cold sterile building every Sunday but rather how you lived your life the entire seven days of the week.

She stood an impressive five foot two inches but in stature she was six foot six and let no man ever stand in her way. She didn't believe in rule books. There was no parenting by Google, Instagram or YouTube back then, you tended to parent based on your inherent skills, instincts and inner beliefs. My mother had this in abundance, a woman who fought every day to take a breath and worked hard to keep herself looking well. She believed that you do not try to make yourself look good for your husband or others but rather you make yourself look good for yourself. She was not gathering 'followers' on social media or using soft filters along with Photoshop to improve her looks. She was a naturally beautiful woman who knew the value of self-resilience and belief.

Make no mistake, my mum was not someone who pampered her children, she was old school and if we crossed the line then you knew you would be reprimanded with the wooden hairbrush. Not that she used it that often but rather it acted as a deterrent. In those days, getting a slap across the legs was not a cause for a child to go rushing to call Child Line. For two reasons, one, Child Line didn't exist and two, there was no phone in the house. I am not advocating corporal punishment here and do not want to get into a debate on the psychology of the impact hitting a child has on them. Those were different times and corporal punishment was the norm not just within families but more so in schools. I can recall many a time getting slapped with a cane in primary school. Indeed, during my five year term in secondary school the beating by the teachers ranged from an instrument of their choice, some used canes, leathers, they even threw the duster at you if you were caught falling asleep. Then there were those Carmelite Brother Teachers who preferred to use their fist or steel toe capped boot to kick you in the shins.

It was a very rare occasion if I did get the blunt edge of my mum's hairbrush. In general, 95% of all beatings were bestowed upon me by the well-educated and highly respected pillars of society, the teachers.

One incident I recall and we laughed many a time about it in adult life with her was when I had done something I shouldn't have. I can't recall exactly what I did but needless to say it was not something that my mum approved of. She had been out, I think at the hairdresser and that was never a good time to upset her. She always came home exhausted from getting her hair done and needed to lie down after, often coughing up blood the following day.

That day she arrived home and was furious at my brother and I. She was wearing a beautiful black velvet jacket and as she went to swipe a slap at me I can still see it in slow motion to this day. Her arm raising, the jacket sleeve stretching and then the noise, oh the noise of velvet ripping is a sound that now even stops me in my tracks. Her jacket ripped and, at that, the thunderous dark clouds came rolling across our house as an eclipse of all normal motherly caring service was suspended momentarily and replaced with a torrent of rage akin to a visit by Lilith the rejected wife of Adam from Jewish folklore.

My brother and I ran like we had never done before up the stairs to the sanctuary of our bedroom. There was no naughty step back in those days. Our aim was to get into our bedroom as quick as possible and pray she was too exhausted to travel up the stairs. The plan worked but a noise we had never heard before or since came bellowing up the stairs like a screech from the depths of hell stating, "Stay in your room and just wait till your father gets home."

Our fear was immense as mum never depended on dad to chastise us. I cried myself to sleep from emotional exhaustion as there was no greater wrong in this world to me at that point in my life than to have upset my mum that much. I recall climbing into my bed and just sobbing my little heart out. I was nine years old and felt that my life was now never going to be the same. The tears came uncontrollably down my face as my body shuddered from the thoughts of hurting my mum so much. How could I have done this to her, she was my saviour in this world that I was finding so difficult to navigate through? When I eventually woke it was dark outside and I could hear my parents talking downstairs. My mum was still upset at what we had done and told my father to go up and deal with 'those boys'.

As he approached our bedroom door we were both terrified. The door handle turned and in he walked. He looked disapprovingly upon the two of us. Not a man who had ever reprimanded us as it was always mum who did so. He had a belt in his hand and our faces turned to the ghostly colour of our death mask. This was going to hurt, how will I cope with it, oh how I wish I could just turn back the clock and not have misbehaved the way I did.

Then the strangest thing happened as he said in a stern voice;

> "I've heard what you boys did and your mum is very upset. She has sent me up here to deal with you both so I am going to crack this belt and then I want you to scream, like you've been slapped with it."

My brother and I broke out into what can only be described as uncontrollable nervous laughter from the sheer relief of getting a pardon and stay of execution. Little did I know that mum had orchestrated the entire scheme as she felt we had suffered enough by staying in our bedrooms and her heart broke too when she heard my crying.

Corporal punishment was regrettably the 'go to' strategy for teachers and parents alike when I was a young child back in the 1960s. The fact that the Department of Education was in support of it and society, as a whole, found it appropriate to allow such beatings to take place within the confines of schools, homes and indeed public places does not mean it was right. That said, it did not turn me into a violent person who reared his children by the force of the hand. I have never found it appropriate that a young child should be slapped or indeed beaten with a weapon of choice by a teacher. For me, violence was always the weaker person's argument, it indicated an inability to have rational constructive debate especially in a school environment. The teachers at that time were seen as the powerhouses and guardians of society's future adults. We were placed under their care to be moulded into a vision of what the elders of the country felt was appropriate. They felt we would succumb to the many vices and temptations that existed and we would have no moral compass. But history has not been kind to the Catholic Church in Ireland and further afield as its seedy secrets of child sex abuse, physical and mental abuse etc. have been unearthed. Once confined to the darkness of hypocritical secrecy, the solid rock that once protected these dark secrets has been rolled away to expose the victims allowing light be shone on their stories as they find their voices. In general from my personal experience those who inflicted such beatings were male teachers who were incapable of controlling a room full of teenage boys without resorting to physical violence. The beatings were severe and not always justified, if indeed beatings can ever be justified. Thankfully the "slaps" I may have encountered at home were few and far between and, in the main, more of a gentle slap and never a beating. But the same cannot be said of those beatings I received in primary and secondary school. If a teacher was to hit a child with their bare fists nowadays they would rightly be prosecuted and jailed for physical abuse. On reflection, I cannot say that the punishments I received are what has made me very much against any form of physical violence. I think my home life has moulded me more that way than anything else as it was a safe loving environment.

School, on the other hand, was a traumatic experience for me and my only aim during my period there was to escape and get away from it as soon as possible. In 1982 corporal punishment was banned in Ireland from schools and it took till 1996 before its use became a criminal offence. The school beatings I encountered did not make me a better person as the same result could have been achieved by engaging with me in dialogue.

My early years in this world were very confused and as you will read later traumatic at times. I had some issues, no I had many issues, that I never truly understood. My world seemed overwhelming and day to day things caused me anxiety and stress that I gradually learned how to cope with but did so through trial and self-survival in a world that, to me, appeared unwelcoming and frightening. My mum would often say to her friends, 'what will happen to Raymond if I pass? Nobody will understand him, he will be lost, he is not meant for this world. He is too gentle, people will bully and take advantage of him, and he needs me.' She was so right, my mum was without doubt my protector from a world that I couldn't cope with. She nurtured and guided me through the obstacles and together we overcame all. Whilst parted we were neither whole or complete.

When I look back as I write this passage I realise just how wonderful she was. To be loved is a gift like no other, but to be loved so much by your mother is a lifelong presence you feel till your last breath.

As mentioned previously, there was no "source" for my mum to reference to figure out how to deal with this child she had given birth to. His needs were many and his wants few. As a child I was unable to traverse a shop that had carpet in it, strange, even weird as that may sound it caused me huge sensory issues. By the age of nine I was still unable to read properly, tying my shoe laces was an impossible task, telling the time was not on my radar and certain foods caused me major issues, scrap that almost all foods caused me issues.

At the time in Ireland which was the 60's and 70's dyslexia, ASD, etc. where unknown terms. Children were just thought to be slow, disruptive or troublesome. It was an era during which the Irish education system ran according to a preconceived concept of what a child's behaviour should be with no exceptions. There was little help for those that needed it and square pegs didn't fit into round holes. But we all know that is not a true statement as it simply depends on the diameter of the round hole compared to the surface measurement of the square.

One story my mum relayed to me many times was she had cooked me fish fingers one day, I ate them all and told her how nice they were. Poor mum thought she had solved this cryptic puzzle of what foods I liked so the next day I got fish fingers again and by the fourth day I proclaimed to her in a self-righteous tone, I said I liked them but that doesn't mean I want to eat them every day!

You have to ask yourself, who else would or indeed could have dealt with a child like me. I know I couldn't but yet this woman, through her own self-belief and sheer determination, did. She had so many challenges to cope with from her own health perspective but still she carried on through to not only help navigate me through life but ensured she was there to do it herself. It is for this and so many other reasons that I see the similarities between her and Vicky Phelan. Both are women who know what is right, have a steely determination and a hunger for life that will not be snuffed out without a fight. When death came calling on my mother's door she sent him packing empty handed many a time. Instead, she would go in her time and when she felt her life's work had been completed.

I would love to say mum had a peaceful and tranquil death but regrettably she had not. For the last six years of her life she suffered with severe dementia. It was a slow stealth like process that silently crept into our lives. In the early years she had moments of lucidity and my father would often find her crying at the breakfast table.

> "Mary what's wrong?"
>
> "Oh Pat, I know I am losing it, I feel I am drifting away from you all. I say nasty things to you and I don't mean to."
>
> "We know you don't mean it Mary, it is ok."

But it wasn't okay, this was not in the script to our life story, this woman had fought all her life to just take a breath and now in her last years she is losing her memories. The one thing she found comfort in whilst sitting in her favourite armchair with her cup of tea in hand was to just reminisce about her family and all the happy joyous moments she could call upon.

They had now been stolen from her, they were being deleted from her memory bank even to the extent we could see at times her struggling to recognise our faces. To sit in front of the woman who has loved and cherished you all your life suddenly struggle to comprehend who you are is a frightening and deeply upsetting place to be. Here in front of me is the woman I owe my life to and I don't say that lightly, she shrouded me in love and gave me an inner belief that I could and would survive this world. She also gave me my self-worth, a sense of being and that my existence mattered not just to her but to the community and indeed the world. And now she was navigating my face like a facial recognition scanner trying to recall who I was but yet at the same time knowing she knew me. I never let her struggle trying to recognise me as I would always put my arms around her and say, 'hello mum how are you today. As always, you are looking beautiful.'

It was now my turn to put those protective arms around her as she had done for me so many times. If her dementia gave me one thing it was the time to repay back all the love, tenderness and reassurance she had provided me with. To cradle your mother in your arms, I mean truly hold her tight like you would your child and stroke her hair as she would snuggle up to you is one of the most long lasting memories you can take away with you from this illness. I do not want to romanticise this illness, it is horrible and I would always tell people that my mother died years before she departed this world, but we have to take something positive out of every negative we find ourselves embroiled within life. We cannot only see the negatives, even in discomfort, pain and yes death there will be positives to take away. For me, I can safely say my mum knew she was loved and I still talk with her every day. By doing so I keep her memory alive. When and where possible I always mention her name. Our lives are short compared to the trees and if we let the wind carry the names of our loved ones across time we honour them and keep them alive as death is temporary like life. Our eternal living lives on in the memories of the next generations as they are the custodians of our legacy that we have given to this world. They are the ones who will bring us to places we never thought we could get to. By simply mentioning my mum in this book in this way I am certain that she will now find her life is slowly beginning to get the recognition and acknowledgments it deserves in places she may never have even visited whilst living.

I have always been fascinated by how people place strangers they will never meet upon a pedestal, and in this world of social media it is escalating to the likes of bloggers and vloggers. Whereas the people they should be in awe of are most likely sitting in a chair opposite them or within their own circle of friends. It is these people who will help you through your darkest moments that will come knocking on your door as they do on all our doors. Life is not simple or indeed easy, it's not meant to be and at some time in your life you will need to call upon friends. When that day comes you will know the true value of someone who cares for you and can be there for you.

This book is written for no other purpose than to shed light in those dark corners we don't feel comfortable going into. It's like when we are young you may think there is someone lurking in the darkness under our bed and just as we are about to drift off into a sleep they will reach out their arm from underneath and pull us into the abyss of where all our anxieties and fears live. But we know there is no one under there, we know that turning on the light won't vanquish them away but somehow when the light is turned on we will gladly climb into that same bed. That's what good friends are like, they are the light that will keep you safe and banish your tormentors and insecurities.

We will all suffer dark moments at some point in our lives, whether that may be the emergence of some traumatic event that happened when you were a child, a family member dying or serious illness. There will be days that we may think light will never visit upon our being again. But it will and the darkness shall evaporate, that is not to say that the darkness will not stay for long periods or revisit often but rather there will always be brighter moments at some stage. We need to embrace darkness as much as we do the light. We need to become comfortable within our own suffering. For us to continually churn out positivity vibes to the universe will not vanquish negativity or indeed the darkness. We need to let people know it is perfectly alright to feel 'down', to feel uncomfortable in our own skin but that we can get through it. It won't be easy, it often won't be immediate and someone telling you how lucky you are won't change that. But we do need to realise the importance of our own lives, not for other's sake but rather for our own sake. We need to mean something to ourselves.

'Are You There Mummy' is a poem I wrote one night having visited my mum. I was lying in bed contemplating all we had been through but more importantly her life and why a woman who suffered with such bad health issues had to have her memories stolen from her by dementia. During that period my mum was still alive but yet she was not, she was unable to engage with her family the way she always had and at times didn't even recognise them. But this is real life, it is not a novel or fairy-tale with a happy ending it is the harsh reality of how our journey can have many challenges but with those challenges comes strength and a finding of one's inner resilience.

I'm sure the reader can tell that I am extremely proud of my mum for the way she coped with what life threw at her, never one to surrender and seek pity but rather stand one's ground and fight for what she believed was right. She instilled in me the *joie de vie,* to see the extraordinary in the ordinary and to appreciate the simple things in life that can make you happy. 'Beauty', she would tell me, 'is all around us if we are willing to open our hearts and eyes to it'.

Money was something she put no value on, she would say it is a means to an end but continually aiming for higher financial rewards can be no guarantee of greater contentment. She would tell me that you are the only person who can truly make you happy, yes those around you can bring happiness into your life but inner peace is found when you are content with who you are and who you have become.

As I write about her in this book I realise just how much she influenced who I am and for those Master Classes I am thankful to her. Our lives are moulded by so many events that happen to and around us.

As a young boy I have so many fond memories that my memory drive needs upgrading. As a young man there was the struggle that ensues when a mother has to let go of their child and allow them the space to flourish in their own environment. It is never easy to truly let go of your children and when they fall not run to fix their cuts and bruises. I too found as a parent I wanted to protect my daughters but in doing so it was not allowing them to experience real life. By standing back you enable them to make their own mistakes and find their way out from the fog of adolescence into the mist of adulthood. Then, as a grandparent, you look on in admiration of your own children becoming parents and seeing how they evolved. Life is, without doubt, a circle and to be able to live on that contour is a beautiful thing.

As a child we were almost in a constant state of readiness for mum's passing as a year never went by when she wasn't admitted to hospital for some new treatment or rest due to infections on her lung. As a young teenager it was never easy to see your mum bent over the side of the bed haemorrhaging blood and then having to pound on her back to help release the gunge that had built up on her lung. My fear was always that I was hurting her but she would simply give me a smile hold my hand and say you need to hit harder to release the phlegm. Those were to me some of the darker moments as I was not and am not someone who believes in any form of physical violence but yet here I was having to, in my eyes, hit my mum hard.

So many times we almost lost her but this was no ordinary woman. As a man in his fifties I look back now on that period of her life and feel frustrated, annoyed and even angry on the cruelty that is life. As an atheist I don't blame any God, but rather simply feel that life is at times a low life form that tries its hardest to snuff the very joy out of living. Dementia is not a disease that is kind to the sufferer or those caring for the patient, it is cruel and stealth like in its approach as it erases their memories like the wiping of a hard drive. At times her dementia stole her dignity and pride; two things she cherished so much in life.

Her last five weeks were spent in St Vincent's Hospital in Dublin. I would travel up every day during that period with my dad to be by her side. And in typical mum's style she even decided on her terms when she would go. We had been forewarned not to go home one night as the end was very close. My brother, dad and I kept vigil over her that night and in the morning she was still with us. We went home momentarily to change and wash, returning in haste. Then, at about midnight, a nurse suggested we go home as it was unlikely she would pass during the night as her breathing had stabilised and they would phone us immediately if things changed.

Once again we said our goodbyes, a kiss on the cheek and gentle hug and most importantly those words I had uttered to her every night, "Goodnight mum, I love you". I lay down on the couch in my parents' house for momentary rest and we persuaded dad to go lie down too. Then after about ninety minutes my dad came down the stairs, ushering me to the car as the hospital had phoned. By the time we got there mum was laying peacefully in the bed, hair brushed, hands laid across her stomach with rosary beads in her grip and a single candle flickering in the room creating a mesmerising dance across the white walls. I looked at my mum's face and then out the window. She was gone, she was never returning and I was now motherless. My dad sat by her side holding her hands, caressing her cheek letting the tears run down his face as he gave his final goodbye kiss to the woman who had loved him and raised his family. As for me, I stared out that window searching for strength but little could be found. Tears ran down my face, a deep throat cry was snuffed out by my inability to allow my emotions unveil. It would have to wait, I needed to be at home, and I needed Selena!

Now five years on from her death I still talk with her daily, I still tell her I love her and I simply let the wind carry her name from my lips to the universe that surrounds us, never forgetting her.

Are You There Mummy?

Sweets discarded, toys abandoned, tears cascading down my face. It hurts oh so bad, make the pain go away, are you there mummy? Safety, warmth, pain dissipates, all is good, wrapped in the comfort of your arms.

Failed exams, fearfulness, pariah of educational acceptance, tears are within. I am sinking in the quicksand of my own inadequacies, anxiety of uncertainty, are you there mum? Hopelessness dissipates; all is good as your words of belief dispel my insecurities.

Abandoned in love, paralysis of emotion ensues. Bleakness descends suppressing the light of hope, are you there mother? Cuppa tea, favourite dinner, home baked apple pie; mother's love is never conditional.

What to do, parenthood is overwhelming, futility at my inability to cope. Failure has once again come knocking on the door of hope, are you there grandma? Understanding, compassion, silence but reassurance in your ever presence of constant stability.

The youthfulness of your heart has cheated the harsh years of your journey upon your face. I touch your cheek, we smile, no words, none needed. I hold you in my arms. You look into my face like only a mother can, as I look back in your eyes I ask myself, are you in there mummy?

Don't wear someone's else's guilt like a wet hessian sack strewn across your body on a Good Friday walking barefoot on the blunt cobbles of life, if you are not guilty of something don't let others attribute that sense of guilt upon you.

CHAPTER 2
SILENCED LAMB

Then were there brought unto him little children, that he should put his hands on them, and pray: and the disciples rebuked them. But Jesus said, Suffer little children, and forbid them not, to come unto me: for of such is the kingdom of heaven. And he laid his hands on them, and departed thence. - Mathew 19:13-15

I think that no one can argue that children are the most vulnerable in society as they are totally dependent on those adults around them to be kept safe. As a young boy I attended a Catholic Primary school and was taught by lay teachers. It is somewhat amazing to me how at times I can vividly recall memories from those years but others are blocked out. If I am to be honest I sometimes find it difficult to recall events from the previous day. My mum used to tell me that my brain was too busy that I forgot the events that were of no relevance. Although we did have a good laugh at my expense many times over the years at my carelessness and sheer "blond moments", (I scratch my head now and think have I just said something non-politically correct in today's world). Once I went to the fridge to get some milk for my cup of tea and poured the milk into my cup, placed the cup in the fridge and walked away with the carton of milk in my hand. My mum and brother just sat silently watching me with a smile on their faces waiting to see how long it would take for me to realise what I had done. My mum declared:

"Oh Raymond, you do make me smile at times."

Then there was the occasion I had received the ultimate prize for the music loving enthusiast that I am, the opportunity to listen to a Sony Walkman before they became commercially available in Ireland. Now my daughters will scratch their head at this point in the book wondering was their father born before electricity was invented. But believe it or not there was a time when the Internet didn't exist, smart phones were things of sci-fi movies and to communicate with someone you generally had to talk face-to-face with them.

However, I digress which is perfectly normal for me. There I was, all of seventeen years old feeling the coolest guy in the world with the Walkman strapped to my belt listening to an album on a tape cassette. I had just bought my mum some flowers and decided to put them into a ceramic vase she had. Now, you have to understand this scene particularly well. The vase was rather large, in the shape of I guess what could be best described as a coffee pot with ceramic flowers carved into the front of it and stood on four legs. My brother, his girlfriend, Selena (my then girlfriend and now wife) and mum were all spectators to this one.

I strut my stuff into the front room to get the vase, headphones on full volume, feeling rather cool and thinking can life really get any better than this moment, listening to music on personal earphones whilst walking around! I went over to the kitchen sink, filled the ceramic vase with water, took it out of the sink and proceeded to walk back to the front room. I noticed everyone looked somewhat stunned and then began laughing uncontrollably. Then I felt it, my leg was suddenly beginning to feel wet (a sensation I would experience many times later in my life, but wait for that bit). I looked down only to notice that there was water all around me on the floor and my jeans were soaked. You guessed it, as I took the vase out of the sink I broke one of the legs off it. My mum being the kind hearted soul she was didn't shout or berate me but rather saw the humour in it and let the situation play out.

So, those types of memories are the happy ones and easy to recall. Then we have the memories that we find that were not so happy and can be equally as vivid for us. Like when I was in primary school, I struggled with so many things and never really feeling like I fitted in, a bit of an outsider and troubled. One of my earliest memories was when I was in junior infants, so I am guessing I would have been about 4 years old at the time. I soiled my pants and the teacher grabbed me by the ears and pulled me out of my seat. I was crying at the pain and standing on my tiptoes in an attempt to somehow relieve it. She scowled me in front of the entire class and made me sit in my soiled clothes till end of class that afternoon. To this day I can still feel the utter embarrassment of my younger self although I was so young and did not have the vocabulary to describe my emotions I guess if I had I would have said I felt demeaned. Corporal punishment was the norm back then but I have to state not all my teachers in primary school were so cruel, for senior infants I had a most kind and loving teacher, think Miss Honey from the book Matilda and you won't go too far wrong visualising what she was like.

Then there was a remarkable teacher who was present in my life from fourth to six class, and who, in my humble opinion, was one of my influencers in life. A teacher who was so advanced in his teaching techniques and understanding of the needs of children who didn't fit into the norms of schooling. I could write an entire book on how he developed my young mind and influenced me right through to this point in my life. Before we completed our primary school years in sixth class every Friday he would play an episode from a documentary on an 8mm projector about drug addiction and, in particular, heroin. He also managed to somehow get hold of the complete history of World War I and II.

But the one that helped me to this day was every Friday afternoon we sat diligently in our desks, a sheet of white grease proof butcher paper was placed in front of us. Why butcher paper, because one of my classmates father's was a butcher, did you really need to ask? We then had our water colour paints and brushes laid in front of us.

> "Okay boys, heads down and rest them on your folded arms, close your eyes and let's start."

I gently lowered my head onto my folded arms, my eyes were shut, not tight because there was nothing to fear. My breathing was calm, and on a sunny day I could feel the heat from the sun rays caressing my body as I sat there. This was escapism, this was what paradise must feel like this was (and is) my happy place. Then it began, our teacher would carefully take the vinyl album out of the cover and then gently place his hands either side of it ensuring not to get any finger marks on the record. He would centre it onto the record player. Now, at this point the excitement was building up within. What record would he play today, what would the sound be like, it began. Inevitably it was a classical music album, Mozart, Bach, Vivaldi were the popstars to be listened to on those Friday afternoons. And no we were not all classical nerds, in fact I think I can safely say at that age this was the only exposure any of us had to classical music.

> "Boys no talking or whispering, I want you all to listen intently and when the music finishes I want you all to paint what you saw in your mind's eye, whether that be an image, a scene or just colours."

The music would start and inevitably I saw colours in my mind. The notes emanating and enveloping the room were like an artist standing at the top of the class spraying carelessly his paint across the walls, floors and ceiling. They were bright, they were bold and they were joyous.

Henceforth my sanctuary became engulfing myself in music to allow me escape the torment of this world. Even to this day there is no greater pleasure for me than to listen to music, attend concerts and go back to being that eleven year old boy cradled in the sun beams listening to those music notes dance across the floor. It was as if I was getting the music fed into my veins through intravenous. 'Who needs drugs when one can have music rushing through your veins' I have often thought to myself.

However, the years spent in first class through to third class were not so happy or indeed kind to me. I was sexually abused during those years by a priest. They are the memories that we lock away in a steel box, place a heavy chain around, secure by a strong padlock and throw away the key. We then take that box to the dark world, where memories crawl around in the stenched swamp soil of our guilt ridden world never to be exposed to the brightness of day. They seep out in the darkness of night when no one can see the pain engrained on our faces so as not to be visible to the world. Oozing out like the festered gunge from a sceptic sore. Spreading across our impaled body on the crucifix of our guilt, hanging listlessly on the subconscious of our anxieties.

But with darkness comes light, and as we traverse the obstacles we encounter on our journey through this life we gather up resistance like a child building up their immune system. My childhood was in my opinion not bad although scattered with challenges it was primarily a loving one due to my family and their ability to vanquish demons from my life that they were unaware even existed. There was a ritual in our house that we never parted without saying, 'I love you'. It was an unspoken ritual, no one ever decided that we should say those words to one another but rather it appeared to organically grow from the seeds of love our parents provided to us.

It's important, I think, that you realise we were not and are not the perfect family. We're not the Brady Bunch. We were as dysfunctional as the next family. There is no perfect family as they only exist in the minds of film and television script writers. We were a real family and I made this point at my mum's funeral during her eulogy. I don't want anyone to think, well it's alright for the Poole's. Sure, they had the ideal upbringing with no challenges. I think by the time you finish reading this book you will realise my life was and is far from perfection. However, the point I would like you all to take away from this book is that yes we will have challenges in our lives and some will seem so overwhelming that we may wonder will we ever get through them. But we do, somehow, somewhere we all muster up the strength to do so if we simply let time pass. For those of you who have faith you may feel that there is help beyond this planet. For those like me who have no religion or faith you, too, can overcome challenges. It's just not divine intervention. ☺

Here is the thing though. Time must pass and we have to let that time pass. I can honestly state here as I am writing this paragraph that my 20 year old self did not think the same way as my 30, 40 or even 50 year old self did. I dare say when I am 60 I will think differently to how I think now too. Life is about gathering those experiences and developing our coping mechanisms to see us through the future turbulent times. No one person has all the answers, in some instances there are no answers, no reasons, it just is and we have to be able to accept that.

We also have to come to terms with the fact that our lives are temporary as is everyone's. We are here for such a short time in the overall scheme of things and we should try to make the best we can out of where we find ourselves. The truth of the matter is we are all terminally ill and the illness that is killing us is life, no more or less than anything else. I am not belittling anyone who has been diagnosed as terminally ill, here, I would never do that especially with my mum's and currently my dad's health issues. However, what I am trying to make you all realise is that you too will die, you know not the hour, day or year.

It is often said when you have an encounter with death or a serious illness that you refocus and start comprehending the true meaning of life. But listen, what if I told you right now you are terminally ill, would you change your life, your behaviour, your outlook? The reality is your life is terminal so come to terms with your impermanence and start living the life you want now as tomorrow may never come. Tell those you truly love that you do, spend time with those who make you smile and happy. And never take anyone or anything for granted, so when they do depart this world you will have few regrets. Note I don't say no regrets because at some stage in our lives most of us will have some regrets but let's make them as few as possible.

Further on in this book I will cover why those three years in primary school were such a challenge for me. But something I will talk about here is the bullying that I am certain at some level we have all encountered in our lives. I was deemed to be a gentle looking child, I guess the term back then would have been soft or even spoiled. We were in no way a wealthy family in monetary terms but we were extremely wealthy in love. As for being 'soft' I guess a better term could be a gentle soul who didn't like to see suffering or cruelty. But for those of you who are parents or indeed even those who are not, you will know that there can be no crueller a group than a pack of young children. They have the capability when gathered in a group to act like a single pack of wolves tracking and hunting their prey. Their words and actions can be crucifying to the poor individual who is the object of their poisoned words and taunts. As a parent we want to safeguard our children against the cruelties of this world but the reality is we cannot always protect them and we have to realise that. Indeed, we have to also accept that at some stage they are the master of their own destiny, they are in control of what happens next and we have to realise that too. It is not easy but we have to let go as we do for all things in life.

I was very fortunate to live in the time I did as the bullying I encountered happened during school hours. Once school was over there was no Internet, no social media or texting so my bullies were restricted by the bandwidth of time spent at the school. Why was I bullied? That is a question you would have to ask the individuals who inflicted their torments and abuse on me. In primary school it was predominantly name calling, and being left out of games etc. I was most definitely not the cool kid in the yard, rather shy and timid would be a better description of me. Don't get me wrong. I did have friends, but they were limited.

During those years I was also suffering another form of abuse that of sexual abuse by a priest. Sympathy is something I have never sought and this book is not about me wearing my hessian cloth sack seeking out glances of pity, there is no pity required or requested. My life was and is good, yes I have challenges but we all have obstacles we must overcome. Some are there because of things that have happened to us, some are there because of how we perceive the world to be and some are not there but we think they are.

Bullying is the lowest form of behaviour and unfortunately it is not restricted to children but rather finds itself seeping into the workplace and indeed the boardrooms of many a corporate establishment. Yes, there may be anti-bullying policies in place but the issue with that is the victims have to report the bullying. For them to do so takes an enormous amount of courage as they tend to find themselves in a coercive position. Safe places and boundaries need to be defined and established but not at the detriment of removing human interaction. We are complex creatures who have a varying degree of proprietary depending on the cultural environment you may find yourself working in or indeed within a multi-cultural team.

I have had the pleasure of working with many teams in different continents and in teams that had a global mix. When working in such environments I had to be always conscious of what is and isn't appropriate in certain regions and cultures. But bullying is the same thing regardless of where you work, and to stamp it out we need teams to unite with one another and look out for each other. It can cause immense stress and mental health issues for the victim and at the extreme level can lead to them feeling there is no escape or safe place.

*There is help out there if you have personally been abused or know of someone who has. You can contact the following agencies in Ireland:

One in Four – 01 6624070 www.oneinfour.ie

ChildLine – 1800 666666 www.childline.ie

Rape Crisis Centre – 1800 778888 www.rapecrisishelp.ie

If you live outside of Ireland you can use Google to locate a local support service in your country. Don't ever feel afraid to reach out and ask for help, although your situation at this point in time may seem helpless to you, there is help and support. The first step on that road to recovery is to seek out help.

Damaged Goods is a poem written about myself as I reflected on my journey up to my late teen years. Always on the outside never quite fitting in with societies preconceived perceptions.

Damaged Goods

Born to a loving family with all the imperfections that exist in a family unit

The runt of the litter the child who could not wait to be born

Too pretty for a boy they said too gentle to be heterosexual

Whispers in the corridors, nudges and sly glances

Damaged goods, soiled through years of physical, mental and sexual abuse by the glistening white collars of societies guardians against Satan

Struggled, stumbled, crawled my way through puberty

Mummy's boy they jeered with the spiteful venom in their tone

Slow, lazy, mentally challenged were the tag lines in school reports

Destined to roam aimlessly through life never to find a professional career they scorned at him

Rise above she whispered, you are my gift to the universe they know not what I know, you are my light shine bright

The imperfections in our life are what make us truly unique, don't hide them but rather celebrate them.

CHAPTER 3
WHO AM I?

Who am I? This is a question I have often pondered. I am an individual who seems to be a contradiction of his very self, I mean I am not a straight line, my thoughts waver between my likes and dislikes they get confused. I like living in the countryside but yet love visiting cities like London, Paris etc. I hate lying in the sun but love the heat on my body, confused.com was designed for me, and it should be my domain name. Whilst attending a course during 2010 at University Limerick we did a weekend session whereby each student performed certain tasks and took a test. I distinctly recall the facilitator not accepting the results of the home test we did as he said it was impossible to get the analysis I got. During the weekend session while our results from an in class profiling exam were being called out each student would go up to collect their personal profile results based on the test scripts they answered. The following conversation ensued in front of the entire class.

"Raymond Poole!"

"Yes, that's me."

"Oh. Hold on. Let me look at those results I remember you."

"OK."

"Hmm, I can honestly say in my 30+ years I have never come across a profile like yours."

"That's nice for you then!"

"You're quite unique."

"Yes I know, my mum always said I was special."

The entire class full of mature students' breakout into laughter. I walk proudly up to collect those results knowing now that my mother was right and this was vindication for all those years when she kept telling school after school that 'Raymond is different'.

When I was about ten I was taken to St John of Gods to be analysed as the school I was attending was concerned about my academic abilities or should we say inabilities. I spent the entire day being analysed extensively separated from my mum and father. Years later, my mother told me that the "specialist" suggested to her that my intellectual growth was being hampered by her because she was loving me too much. They suggested that she buy herself a stuffed teddy bear and whenever she felt like hugging me she should hug the teddy bear. Needleless to say no teddy bear was ever purchased and my mum and I continued hugging one another until she took her last breath at the age of 80. Not once did the education system stop to think that they could be the issue in the way they were teaching me. Back then, ASD and Dyslexia were not known or recognised and my education suffered because of their lack of foresight. Furthermore, the fact I was sexually abused over a period of 2-3 years did not help matters. As you read in later chapters of the book you will see how that came out of the closet to impact my journey with cancer.

But this book is not simply about my childhood and journey into adulthood. It is about an unfinished life and the evolution of me as a person. All these episodes that happened throughout my life are threads in the fabric that make me and their interwoven experiences formulate how I approach things in life, especially my journey with cancer. We are complex creatures and to simplify who we are does a disservice to us. To understand anyone fully you must understand their journey, the encounters, challenges, failures and successes they have had.

If I was to describe myself I would liken me to a tree standing isolated in a field during the autumn with its leaves blazing brightly in autumnal colours. Preparing to shed my foliage and stand proud and naked before the oncoming winter storms against the grey thunderous clouds knowing that spring will be just around the corner. As in nature, we first must die back into the ground before we can return stronger, brighter and more resilient during the coming spring.

When I die I want there to be no major regrets. I have lived a very happy and fruitful life full of enjoyment but, more importantly, love. Yes, I have had challenges and encounters I would rather had not happened. But overall my life has been a good one. When we are young we can become obsessed with collecting sparkly foibles that we think will bring us satisfaction and joy. The reality is most things that can be purchased cannot bring joy into our lives. True contentment and real joy is brought from what is around you and is generally free. The reciprocal love from your partner, the joy of children, the laughter with friends. Experiencing nature and observing the beauty that lies within it. Sitting on a lazy sunny day watching the world slowly go by feeling the sun on your body. The sheer rush of adrenaline that runs through your veins when your fingers touch the hand of the person you have a crush on for the first time. These and many more things in life are what will bring you true joy.

If any parent has a child who is struggling within the education system and they are labelled as having a learning disability I hope you take some solace from this book. Just because we may not fit into the system that is geared towards teaching the masses and not inclusive of the few don't lose heart. Every single person in the world has ability, it may not be of the type that is readily graded through state exams. But we all have something to offer this world, our journeys need to be different so we can shine. Have trust in your child's ability but more importantly in your instinctive judgement for your own child and your ability to be a good parent.

I always recall when our youngest daughter was a baby and she had a kidney issue. We spent many a night in Harcourt Children's Hospital. One day, the consultant came into her room, he had his team with him and asked would we mind if they reviewed our daughter's case. We consented to them doing so. Student after student gave their independent analysis of what they thought was wrong with our daughter by reading her chart. When they all completed their reporting he looked at them all, took a deep breath and softly spoke to them. In summary, he suggested that the next time rather than simply reading medical charts they talk with the child's mother as he said no one knows a child better than their mother.

As a parent we can doubt our ability to know what is best for our children but if we go with our instinct we will rarely do wrong by them. I was as confused being a parent as I was a child and now as a Pappy I am equally confused. I don't place pressure on myself anymore by having to know the answer to ever problem. I am okay with getting things wrong and exposing my vulnerability. To progress we have to expose ourselves, take risks and be comfortable with our failures. Success is the child born out of failures.

Do you know who you are?

When we look back on our lives we won't immediately recall the challenges but rather the times we laughed, loved and were loved. Make sure they are plentiful.

CHAPTER 4
THE BIG C

Cancer, such a small word but yet has the capacity to stop you dead in your tracks (literally) and cause more mental stress than physical stress if allowed. In July 2016 at 53 years young it is something that had never given me a moment's concern. I mean after all I was a non-smoker and never drank any alcohol, clean living, relatively carefree individual walking between life appointments like any other. I was working at the peak of my professional career having spent all of 2011 and 2012 in South Africa working as a Project Manager on a large scale project implementing a project controls system.

Following this assignment I was in demand and set my sights on working with one of the biggest oil companies in the world at their offices in Baku, Azerbaijan where I spent the next two years. In 2015 I worked remotely from my offices in Blessington, Wicklow, Ireland managing a global rollout for the same client. Then 2016 came and I found myself working on yet another large scale implementation for a government body in the UK. Things were good we were riding a wave the likes of never before experienced. All my hard work, dedication and continued professional development had come together like an El Neno (perfect storm). I was at the pinnacle of my career and things were looking secure for the future. A decision was made to purchase our own offices, renovate them for expansion to be able to take advantage of the growth we were experiencing and prepare for the imminent upturn in the home economy in Ireland. I was feeling confident, this was what I had spent the last decade plus preparing for. It was there to be taken and I was ready to grasp it with both hands as were our team.

My routine during 2016 was to fly out to the client offices on a Monday morning catching the 06:50 Ryanair flight to Bristol and then returning home on a Thursday night on the 21:10 flight. It was a rough routine which I found tiring as it meant waking on a Monday morning at 04:00 to be ready for the taxi at 04:45. Then, most Thursdays the flight home was delayed and I arrived in the door after 23:30. Friday was a normal workday from the office in Blessington and then Sunday was preparing to depart on Monday morning again. My tiredness was understandable and I thought nothing of it. I had been used to working away from home, whilst in Baku I was on a 7 week rotation which meant I worked a 7-day week for 7 weeks and then came home for a week. This was the career I chose and I knew I had a limited time that I would be capable of doing such assignments.

I had a regular health routine since my mid-40s which was every year usually during the summer months I would visit my GP for blood tests and general check-up. I recall when I was in my 40s requesting my bloods be sent for a PSA test, in fact, at that age my GP thought I was being a little precautious but agreed to get them done nonetheless for me as my father had been diagnosed with cancer of the colon at that time.

Without getting too scientific a PSA blood test measures a protein made by the prostate gland called prostate specific antigen (PSA). The level of PSA in the blood stream can rise if you have prostate cancer but it can rise for other reasons as well, so a raised PSA does not necessarily mean you have prostate cancer. The normal level of PSA changes as you get older.

In July 2016 I did just that like every other year, no new symptoms or concerns on my behalf. My libido was down but I had put that down to the long hours I was working and travelling plus stress from projects I was working on, along with maintaining the office in Ireland and ensuring we were all kept busy.

In November 2015 we were on vacation with the family (four generations) in Orlando, Florida visiting Disney. An office unit in my hometown of Blessington, Co. Wicklow caught my eye and whist on vacation we put in a bid for it which was accepted. We were ecstatic, at last we had secured our own premises and could renovate the building the way we had always wanted to. No expense was spared, the design was to the highest quality and on numerous occasions clients would refer to their astonishment at the interior design of the building. It was often mentioned that it would not be out of place as being described as a Google or Apple satellite office, it was that good. We were proud of our achievements and the team were proud of where they worked and we all enjoyed the rewards of the company doing well.

During the loan negotiations with the Bank they suggested I take out a serious illness insurance policy, not bothered either way I agreed to this as I didn't feel ill but what caught my eye was if I should die the business loan would be paid off. As the sole earner in our home I didn't want to leave any financial concerns for my wife in the rare event that something would happen to me. Little did I know that the decision I made that day when signing the insurance policy would keep me from the breadline and bankruptcy.

We moved into our office in May 2016 and I was due to stay on the project in the UK till at least end of the year. I had undergone a medical for the insurance company to secure the business loan for the office so I was in no hurry with my visit to the GP. Everything in life seemed fine, other than the tiredness but who wouldn't be tired with that schedule I had, it was hectic to say the least.

June 2016 came and went, then in July I made an appointment to go visit my GP to get my bloods done. During the visit everything seemed fine nothing out of the ordinary and I had only just passed a medical earlier in March for the insurance company so I was happy with life and how I felt.

The phone rang,

> "Hello, Raymond speaking."
> "Hi Raymond, we have your blood results back and everything seems fine but your PSA count is up, not majorly but slightly, I would like to do another

blood test in four weeks. Nothing to concern yourself about as PSA is not a strict indicator of anything to be concerned about but nonetheless let's do another test."

"No problem, I will schedule it for early August."

I can honestly say that telephone conversation never gave me a second thought, 'PSA sure that could be anything and anyway I know lots of people who have a high PSA and it didn't mean anything. I was not peeing during the night and no blood in semen so I'm good, or so I thought.'

August arrived and as planned I went back to my GP for the blood test, this time the phone call had a more concerned voice over it.

"Hi Raymond, we have your bloods back and your PSA has risen from 9.0 to 10.0 Not a major jump or even a very high count but nonetheless it is an increase. I would like to do an examination can you schedule an appointment for next week."

"No problem, I will see you then."

I hung up the phone and realised that this is "the examination" every man dreads, it's going to be an internal one. Not my first time for such examinations as I have had colonoscopies before and when a teenager there were issues with my digestive system so many an enema and flushing out of the bowel back then. 'I will be fine' I kept telling myself. It cannot be any worse than what you have gone through before, all will be good.

The appointment came and, sure enough, all was good no real hurt or discomfort just messing in my head getting an internal examination. I tried very hard to rationalise things, I would say to myself what are you going on about sure women have to get examined internally a lot more, get over yourself, stop being such a whinge bag. I hadn't realised at that point that it was not the internal examination itself that was the issue but rather the underlining current that had stayed dormant for decades was awoken. It would brim to the surface over the next number of years as I went through many an internal examination and biopsies.

I should have known from past experience with my wife when she had a breakdown due to being a victim in recurring raids in the building society branch she worked in, eleven raids to be precise. It is not necessarily a reoccurrence of the incident that brings the murky waters from the depths of your past hidden in the deepest crevices of your memory to the surface. It is hard to explain to someone who has not gone through a similar experience just how it impacts you. People often wonder how can you now in your mid-50s be reliving something that happened to you almost 50 years ago, why has it not caused you issues before now. To be honest I don't know the answers to those questions, I could research them but I am not interested in the reason why as I know it just does happen.

The way I try to explain it is this. When I stand in front of you now a 50 something year old man you hear an adult talk about being abused as a child but if I asked my grandson aged 6 to stand in front of you and relay the same experiences you would be horrified. The injustice of such things happening to such a young child would appal you and you would have the deepest sympathy for that child.

However, we rarely speak of these issues as a child for many reasons, one being we don't have the vocabulary to explain what is happening to us. We don't realise what is happening to us and we have been told not to by the adult perpetrator. Think about those few things for just a minute, let them sink in and then you will perhaps understand just a small miniscule amount on why we don't mention anything as a child.

Then as an adult we spend our life begging for forgiveness from our younger self for what happened to us. Move on 50 odd years and you are in an examination room being told to pull down your trousers and your pants, lie on your side, pull your knees up to your chin and breathe calmly while someone places their finger inside your anus. It doesn't physically hurt so don't worry about that but every examination peeled back a layer of my resistance, it slowly lightened the weight on the anchor that had kept those thoughts and images deeply buried in the depths of my memory. Slowly, as time progressed and more and more examinations along with biopsies occurred, the anchor would snap and the reliving of my past would come flooding back engulfing me in a tsunami of an emotional wave.

As I wrote this book the recollection of some of those events that occurred during that time in my childhood came flooding back. The following is an account of just one of those experiences.

The sun was beaming in through the window on my back as I sat quietly playing on the floor in my home with toy soldiers recreating a battle scene along the colourful floral pattern carpet lost to my surroundings such was the intensity of my enjoyment. My play was abruptly interrupted by the buzzing noise from the doorbell. It was one of my school mates at the door, my breathing became erratic, and tears began to form as I welled up with fear knowing what was to come. I ran into another room clinging to the chair begging my mum not to let me go swimming. She tried her best to calm me with reassurance that I would be fine, telling me that my friends will be there too, and how much I liked them.

I let go of the chair and my swim bag was handed to me. Mum kissed me and gave me a big hug saying 'you'll be fine Raymond and when you can swim properly mummy and daddy will go watch you'. Little did she know that it was not the swimming I was afraid of but the priest who was allegedly teaching us how to swim.

I walked to his car with my head down, never looking back as I knew if I did I would simply run into the house and I had to be brave in front of my school friends.

There was always about four of five of us who were the 'the chosen ones' to be selected like the prize winners of a competition. How cool and lucky were we, off in the car with this priest. We were his favourites! Our destination was a swimming pool.

We would be told to jump in the pool and, for some, there was excitement, screams and playfulness. My memories are not so happy. I was always the one selected to be 'rubbed down and dried off' by him, obviously swimming trunks had to be removed to dry me off properly or so he would insist.

This same priest was assigned to prepare us all for First Communion and in order to prepare for that we had to do confession. He would take us one by one into a room where we would have 'open confession', my confession typically was told while placed on his lap and he would fondle me. Even writing this now I can smell his stenched tobacco breath and sense the touch of his hands on my innocent body. Here was I supposed to be asking for forgiveness to his God for sins a seven year old committed whilst he was sexually abusing me.

But this was our little secret, how many times have we heard that in the media about these perpetrators. They preyed on the young, innocent and vulnerable. Their God was one of Satan and the orders that protected them were

Satan's congregation. But society at that time had a role to play too even political parties. Always bowing to their whims never questioning or doubting their purpose in life.

Young girls went missing from families off to mother and child homes, launderettes were run by societies discarded innocents. Their lives were not worthy of being saved their children were a black scourge on this catholic land, but none of them ever thought how the mother of their God was an unmarried woman.

We ask questions of how concentration camps could have existed during the Second World War but yet we never questioned how an entire society turned blind eyes on their own children, deafened themselves to the squeal of so called illegitimate childbirth and no one knew!

But now my generation is opening that Pandora's Box, performing the exorcism on the exorcists. And even now some look down on us for talking openly about the injustice that was performed upon us. They think we seek attention and ask why now, why wait so long to talk openly about it? The reason is simple. We must do so, we have to give voice to that innocent child, we have to let them know it was not their fault and we must prevent this from happening again.

I often wonder what would have happened if it had never happened, if my childhood had been safe, if my innocence had not been stolen from me. *I Never Knew I Could Say No* is a small poem I wrote to my younger self asking for forgiveness and I present it to you but more importantly I dedicate to my 6 year old self to whom I am eternally sorry for not acknowledging his pain and suffering adequately before now.

Poetry to me is stripping naked the soul onto the starkness of a blank page stained by the ink of life's journey. It is not necessarily about rhythm and rhyme. Whether you are a Shakespearean literate or like me fumbling through one's limited vocabulary. Poetry is a conduit to explain something you feel deeply emotional about but may not otherwise be able to divulge or indeed say out aloud. It is wearing the emperor's clothes but while you are fully clothed, you are exposing your vulnerability in the hope that others will gain from your words and experiences.

When you read the below, don't think of the 50 something year old author but rather reflect on the child he once was, look at your children, niece, nephew, grandson, brother or sister and hear them say these words. Then reflect upon what you have just read.

I Never Knew I could Say No…

Innocence raped, trust mutilated, emotional blackmail

I was but seven summers through my childhood when he came overshadowing my innocence

The pureness of the white collar was drowned by the blackness of his robes and soul

Trust was engrained through society's blindness of his stature

He stood for purity, holiness and self-sacrifice

No one told me that I was to be the sacrificial lamb

His hands soft from the lack of hard labour, crawled across my pure innocent skin

His years were three decades or more; respect your elders I heard

My body shivered, trembled at his touch, my innocence was been stolen

I could not run, my tear ducts dried up like the savannah, oh please make it stop

It will be our little secret he whispered into my ear through his tobacco stenched breath

I cried myself asleep not knowing why but sensing it was wrong, I never knew I could say no…

We are not brave but rather resilient, we chose not this path but now that we find ourselves on it we will persist as persistence will erode the cobbles of doubt and from their shattered pebbles we will create self-worth.

CHAPTER 5
FALSE HOPES

The issue with the male species, especially the Irish one, is that we are for want of a better description The Emotionally Constipated Irish Male. In saying this I speak very much of my generation and those born before me and up to the 1980s. We grew up being taught that to show our inner feelings and vulnerability was a weakness but yet our very strength can be visible through that weakness, that openness, vulnerability or as a recent national broadcaster asked me, 'Raymond are you one of these touchy feely guys?'

Males are taught from a very early age that they should behave in a certain way, we hear things like, 'big boys don't cry', 'Only sissies cry', 'don't be such a girl', 'man up'. These antiquated sayings still exist but now we hear the millennial generation male being depicted as too touchy feely, but yet if they are that way is it not because of the parenting of the generation who describe them as this? There is irony in there if you look not even too closely.

I simply talk about these issues here to try and provide some context to how and why I behaved in the manner I did when diagnosed with prostate cancer and how I went on that journey. Everything we do in life tends to be referenced back to prior experiences, how we react, what we have as a measuring stick, or look at the future to. For me, my journey with prostate cancer was very much pixelated by my life's journey to that point. My life skills, resilience, my fears, my desires and my resistance to allowing the disease dictate to me rather than me to it.

For instance, what if I had never being abused, would my journey have been easier? I have no doubt it would. However, in my mind I would speak to myself and say, you survived worse, you came through bigger challenges and you will beat this.

As my dad would say to me, 'Son, nothing's ever so bad that it couldn't be worse!

Your life is not over and there is still much to be done and lots you have to offer this world.' That determination gave me hope for the future but I also knew that life is terminal, it will end one day and we are not always forewarned as to when that time is. I had to dig deep and pull myself through this disease, but to do so I had to do something that I rarely ever did in my adult life and that was to become selfish.

Following the examination by my GP in August 2016 it was decided that I would follow up with an urologist. Once again, an appointment was made and we found ourselves sitting across a dark hardwood desk answering questions about any symptoms I may have had. It was a short conversation as I had none other than what was showing up in my PSA results.

Then, that moment when I am once more told to sit up on the bed, pull my trousers and pants down knees to chin and the lubricated finger was inserted. No pain just abnormal sensation and another small chip away at the anchor holding those memories of sexual child abuse allowing them to creep closer to the surface. My wife was with me and, as someone who also experienced child sexual abuse, she was very much aware of the impact these continuous examinations could have on my mental health.

She had in her 30's suffered the ultimate blow when she had her breakdown and a full 12 months of therapy followed for her. She knew the difficulty that such a journey could play on one's mind, whilst impacting their personal and physical relationship with their partner. We had been here before and for me during that journey together, the most devastating moment was when she said to me. 'You know I love you, but I no longer know who I am or who I will be at the end of this journey, I am not even certain I will love or want you.' That night she spoke those words to me as she cried herself to sleep I felt like I was on death row never knowing whether I would get a pardon or if it was the lethal injection for our love. To this day she has lost recollection of that conversation but it is engrained in my mind. At this point in our relationship she was now worried for my mental wellbeing, I was/am the sole earner in our household. She cannot work due to her anxieties and depression. I can only imagine the fear that was rushing through her mind at this stage. She was consumed by the thought I may have cancer but equally concerned that the examinations would lead me on a spiralling downward journey in to the abyss of the darkness where lost souls wander aimlessly seeking refuge but no hope exists.

For my part, I was oblivious to these concepts, my abuse was way off my radar, my immediate concern was hoping that cancer did not exist. After all, I never smoke or drank alcohol, never took any sort of recreational drugs and my eating habits were not exactly ideal but far from being bad. I was not obese and my health in general was of reasonable quality.

> "Pull up your pants and trousers now Raymond and come sit down and we have a chat. Well, there was nothing I could feel, your prostate does not seem enlarged but to be safe let's do further investigations by taking some biopsies."

Now at this juncture I would like to say that since my tests I have done some online research and found doctors who say that an MRI is a better course following high PSA levels as with new technology they can more accurately see if there are any abnormalities. Biopsies are not always accurate even though the size of where you are taking the biopsies from is that of a walnut.

So my biopsies were scheduled for 05-DEC-2016. I was to attend early that morning and the procedure should take no more than 20 minutes. The main thing was I was to be accompanied by someone who could drive me home and Selena had agreed to accompany me, well more insisted than agreed.

We were scheduled to be at the clinic for 08:00am and arrived on time. I went into the reception area, gave my name and completed the usual forms. I was ushered over to some seating in an open and airy atrium.

It was a nice waiting area, people were starting to arrive at work and slowly the place became busy. An elderly gentleman caught my eye because his trousers were frayed at the helm. He looked like a farmer and I wondered if he too was in for biopsies. Then I heard, "Mr Poole please come this way."

We were brought into a very small waiting room, the walls were painted white and there was no windows in it but at least they had a radiator. I was worried I would want to pee during the procedure, so quickly went to the toilet to make certain my bladder was empty. A nurse dressed in operating theatre robes came into the room, "Mr Poole follow me please." We walked along a corridor and then she stopped. She asked if the procedure had been explained to me, I said it had and then handed me a consent form to sign. I then followed her to a room that to me at the time appeared to be a very large operating theatre, my consultant greeted me, he too was dressed in his theatre robes. There was a table at the far side of the room with those large circular lights overhead. "One minute and I will be with you, just sit up on the table for me." He worked away at his computer which was located on a desk in the far corner of the room, it struck me as unusual to have such a desk in a room where one would undertake biopsy procedures. Anyway who was I to argue, he was the consultant.

> "OK Raymond let's start. You will feel the probe go up inside you and then I need to move it around to locate the area I want to take biopsies from, once I take a sample you will hear a click, but try and just relax."

'Relax, are you for real!' But relaxed I tried as to not would only make things worse. It was not painful but more in one's head than anything else. Every time that clicking noise occurred I jumped slightly. I mean how could you not, this was not natural but I kept telling myself what I use to say when I was a teenager getting examinations. 'No matter how upsetting or painful it may be now it will end and when it does it is only a memory. You can get through this, you are better than this procedure, it will not break you and you can beat it.' I lost count of the clicks when we passed twenty, all I could think of was there any of my prostate left!

"OK Raymond, that's it we are all done you can get dressed, just get up slowly as you may be dizzy." I turned around to lie flat on the bed and as I did I saw the consultant was now back at his desk dictating notes. A nurse walked through the room and that guy who I thought was a farmer was suddenly in the room also wearing theatre robes carrying manila files. Really? Was this hygienic? Should someone be walking through a theatre with manila files in their hand? What about a bit of privacy, should any of these people be in here as I am still getting dressed?

> "Raymond who is here to take you home?"
>
> "Selena, my wife is, doctor."
>
> "Ah that's fine, just take it easy for the rest of the day. You may have blood in your urine for a few days and in your semen for a few weeks but nothing to be worried about."
>
> "Will I be ok to fly to Bristol tomorrow morning as I am currently on assignment over there?"
>
> "Yes, I don't see any issues with that."

We drove home, not talking much in the car, I was tired and Selena knew I needed my space. More times than not

Selena can read me better than I can read myself, she knew what I was still ignorant to, this was all having an impact on me due to my childhood.

When I arrived home we took things easy and when I peed I sure did have blood in my urine but we were forewarned, this was only to be expected so nothing to concern myself about, or so I thought.

But let's be honest here. looking down into the toilet bowl and seeing a dark red colour is not a natural sight and I did have concerns. However, although it was a natural occurrence post procedure I was not aware that what I was looking at was an early warning sign and I should have been heading straight back to hospital. You will read further on in this book how we should be looking at Rosé wine in the toilet bowl and not Claret wine but I will leave that experience for further in the book.

Tuesday morning came and I felt relatively well considering the procedure from the day before. I caught the first plane out to Bristol as usual went straight to the client site and spent the day working and prepping for an important meeting on Wednesday morning. When I got back to the hotel that evening I was feeling a little under the weather and still peeing a dark red colour but had my dinner and watched a small bit of television before falling asleep.

On Wednesday I woke, felt as if I was getting a bad cold almost flu like. Body was most certainly not firing on all cylinders. I walked the short distance to the office as I always did every morning, it took me bit longer than normal, some 20mins. I attended the meeting but suddenly my energy levels drained, my shirt became damp from sweat and my temperature started to rise. I knew things were not looking good. I felt as if I was unable to function and upon returning to my desk my colleague took one look at me and said, 'you need to go back to the hotel you look a fright'. I duly cleared my desk and walked back to the hotel. Every step I took felt like I was doing so at half my normal step stride, my bones ached and I felt like the short journey was a marathon. I walked straight through the lobby not noticing anyone or anything. At last I reached my room, turned the door handle and entered, made my way to the bed and fell down onto it and went unconscious.

My phone was vibrating, it was dark out and I was disorientated, suddenly I became aware of my surroundings and realised I had fallen down onto the bed some 4 hours prior. I stumbled to grab the phone and answer it. It was

Selena, she sounded concerned as she had been trying to phone me all day. I explained that I was feeling unwell and had flu like symptoms. My biggest concern at this point was that I was passing so much blood in my urine and had a very high temperature but yet I knew I was unable to move off the bed or make it to a hospital. Selena had contemplated getting a flight over to me but there was none to be got at this late hour. I reassured her by saying I would be flying home tomorrow and she was not to worry. We agreed this was the best option but that she would phone the hospital in the meantime to see if they could recommend anything.

The phone went silent, I was once again alone in a dark hotel room in Bristol unable to move feeling exhausted beyond belief and aching all over. I just wanted to curl up in a foetus position cuddle into my wife and have her hold me gently whilst whispering into my ear, "it will be OK love, and we will get through this." But right at this point I didn't feel safe, secure or sure of myself anymore. The past was slowly making its journey back up to the surface, it had been hidden deep like nuclear waste surrounded in so much emotional resistance that it was never intended to come forth again.

But here I was alone and scared, my younger self was crying at the door to get out but I couldn't hear him. He had laid alone in the darkness for so long, silently being dutiful never uttering a murmur, never seeking attention, always being the dutiful child and keeping those secrets like he was told to. But he needed comfort, he needed to feel a warm embrace, be told it is OK none of this was his fault. I had neglected him for so long, and now he was stumbling his way through the darkness seeking me out, not to shame me or scowl me but rather to allow me to forgive myself.

We are one, we are the same, and we are both tormented and tortured by our past. We feel each other's hidden pain from the shame of what took place but that shame was not ours to be worn but we needed one another to realise that and yet we kept one another apart.

My thoughts were interrupted by the phone buzzing again. It was Selena, she had contacted the hospital where the biopsy procedure had been undertaken and they were suggesting I go straight to a hospital. However, I explained to Selena that I could hardly lift my head off the pillow and that I just needed to rest, I ended the phone call by reassuring her I would not die that night.

As I hung up on the phone I knew I could not keep that promise. I felt absolutely terrible but all I could manage to do was change into my bed clothes, curl up in the bed and go to sleep, for how long I was not certain but I just wanted to close my eyes. As I did I saw my mum. Oh, how I missed her now more than ever. She was the woman who was my safe harbour as a child and right this minute I felt like I was back in childhood and just wanted a warm comforting embrace. Slowly I fell asleep.

Once again I was woken to the buzzing of my phone. It was, you guessed, Selena again. At this point the concern in her voice was palpable and I knew she was truly panicking. Somehow in my state of sheer exhaustion and delirium I managed to leave her thinking I was capable of making the flight on my own and that all will be good. The reality was I didn't know how I was going to manage to get to the airport let alone manage the flight and the taxi ride to the house.

The journey home was like none other I had experienced. The flight was delayed, I was exhausted and it was cold, wet and miserable out. The dark grey of the clouds only reflected how my demeanour was. I was dark, I was grey, I was Eeyore! I managed to get myself on the plane without grabbing attention from the flight attendants in case they told me I looked too ill to fly. The plane landed in Dublin and no happier a homecoming I had ever experienced. I was home on Irish soil where my family was and my heart was bursting with relief. I had made it, somehow, somewhere I had mustered up the energy to make the journey home. It was a homecoming like no other.

I walked as quickly as my body could take me through Terminal 1 to be greeted by my taxi driver, normally a chatty man he knew something was amiss and allowed me a quiet and solitude journey home. No polite conversation, no politics chit chat, no news update just silence. Selena was waiting at the door as we pulled up, she was visibly shook when she saw me and rushed me to bed. I was trembling and sweating profusely, all she wanted to do was get me to a hospital but I argued that they would leave me sitting on a trolley. I was distressed, disorientated and not acting rational.

A council of the highest delegation of the female Poole clan took place that night between Selena and my two daughters, a plan was put into place as to how they would get me to hospital the next morning. During the night my temperature rose so much so that Selena had to change the sheet and my bed clothes as I had soaked it from sweat. At day break I was ushered to get dressed, no arguments and put into the car. I was driven straight to hospital where the triage nurse looked into my eyes with such care and empathy I felt safe, unknowing to her she had released me from the anchor weighing me down into an oblivion of despair. They ushered me into a cubicle where a doctor came to visit me, she looked so angelic with her strawberry blond red hair just like my younger daughter. Doctors came and went but my inner being had left my body at that stage. I was sitting on the end of the bed observing the goings on, I wasn't dying but felt removing myself from the scene worked best for me it was my copping mechanism I had taught myself as a young boy. If I was not present and an alter ego kicked in then things were not happening directly to me but rather a shell of my being.

I compare it to a reptile shedding their skin, they discard it giving a sense of rebirth to itself in its new shiny coat, that's what I was attempting to do. If I could just leave those skins to the elements they would fade into the past and I could move forward. I heard Selena talking, I could see her and my eldest daughter but I couldn't answer, not properly. They left me momentarily and the doctor returned. At this point all I wanted to do was close my eyes and I truly didn't care if I never opened them again. I was in too much discomfort and the energy had been drained out of my body as if a vampire had sucked the very life from my veins.

She was a kind hearted doctor who was tender with her touch, her smile was soothing to my aches. She had to conduct an internal examination and apologised for doing so. For the first time ever the examination caused me pain, she apologised and said that I would be moved to a room very soon.

I looked at my fingers, they were pale, my nails had no colour but appeared grey, and my skin seemed to lie listlessly upon my body. I started to shake uncontrollably, Selena came back just then and placed an extra blanket over me. Sitting by my side she tenderly stroked my hand speaking ever so gently to me trying to reassure me that all would be fine. Why was everyone saying I will be fine so much, am I that sick, am I dying, what is wrong with me. These and many more thoughts flooded through my head, it was beginning to hurt, and I just wanted it all to stop.

I was put into a room on my own, don't recall much after, other than as the Consultant was leaving the room I overheard him say.

"If that infection spreads over night get him straight into ICU."

That was the last thing I heard coherently that night, soon after I fell asleep and throughout the night recall nurses tending my intravenous drip, taking temperature and blood pressure. Little did I know at this point that this was the start of a journey I never thought I would have to take.

The next number of days were a blur, I recall continuous antibiotics being pumped into my body and at one point having the most horrendous migraine, my vision was blurred and in particular I recall the nightlight over the door that would never go off. Why, I thought to myself, would they put such a light in a room, it penetrated my head like a spear been driven slowly through my head piercing me agonisingly.

As my energy returned it was explained to me that I had contracted an infection from the biopsies taken earlier in the week at the other hospital. At first I was angry as was Selena. I mean I went into hospital for a simple procedure and now I found myself critically ill. Little did we know that later we would reflect on this and be thankful that I had contracted the infection, it was without doubt another 'What If' moment in my life.

During my eleven days in hospital the doctors fought tirelessly to find an antibiotic concoction that would kill the infection and as you can see from me writing this book they were successful. The care I received throughout my stay was first class and the respect, dignity and affection shown was without doubt beyond the call of any pay cheque. What these medical professionals did was engrained in their being, no one teaches you this in any university or college. I knew I was at last now in safe hands. The eleven days were spent getting drips, blood pressure, scans and blood tests done almost every day. My arm was now beginning to resemble that of a drug addict who was shooting up every day and in a way I was shooting up - but on life saving medication. Many times my veins collapsed and there was pain when washing out the cannula. But that pain paled into insignificance compared to what I had experienced before being admitted.

My body was now beginning to recover from the trauma but my mental health was being chipped away, the effects of all this was slowly unravelling the secrets of the abuse that had occurred decades ago, the impact of which I would not fully feel till post-surgery. At this point in time I was totally naïve of any further treatments being required. The train that I thought had come to its final destination on this leg of life's journey was simply at an intermittent stop enroute.

Selena phoned the hospital for my results where I had had my biopsies done. It was good news, no it was great news all 25+ biopsies were non-cancerous, I was in the clear I had no cancer. Oh, this was going to be a Christmas to celebrate, the relief we felt was almost indescribable. It was as if we had being living under an oppressive weather front that was slowly draining the energy from our body and sucking out any sense of positivity we could ever have had. But now this, the news that there was no cancer not even one of the biopsy samples indicated any cancer, this was a celebration, a Christmas that would be remembered for many years to come. My birthday falls on Christmas day and although I would only be discharged from hospital on 19-DEC we were going to celebrate it. Christmas is Selena's favourite time of year, she is the original Mrs Claus, no effort is left unturned to decorate the house and light up the little faces of our four grandchildren when they come to visit Pappy and Gram's house.

Christmas came and went so fast that I can honestly say I was not present in the moment. My body was still healing from the infection and my mind from the near encounter I had just had with cancer.

Normal service resumed in mid-January whereby I was back on the Monday morning flight but now I was coming home on a Wednesday evening and working from Blessington on Thursday and Friday. The client was very understanding and I needed to work in order to generate revenue for the company as I had missed a considerable number of days due to the hospitalisation and recovery period.

Burnout is a term we have all heard about but make the assumption we have all the bases covered so that will never happen to us as that sort of thing only happens to others. Those were my very thoughts in relation to Prostate Cancer, sure that only happens to old men, I will be in my late 70s before I even have to think about that and even if I do contract it, it's not that serious an illness. How wrong was I? The one thing I have discovered about having cancer is that it is not just your body that is affected but your mind, your mental health, your partner, your family and most definitely your business. This then creates a loop affect whereby it impacts your stress levels that, in turn, impact on mental health and wellbeing.

My life's journey continued as mentioned above from early January but in mid-February I woke one Saturday morning and tried to get out of the bed but fell back onto it due to a shooting pain in my leg and hip. Once again I became mentally paralysed as to what was happening to this vessel of a body of mine who up till now had been so reliable. Visits ensued back to the A&E only to end up with having to attend physiotherapy for five weeks to get me to a stage whereby I could walk again comfortably. Initially, I had to sleep on a couch, the pain was that bad when I either stood up or lay down. But like all intermittent inconveniences in life it passed and once again I felt I was indestructible and returned to my crazy routine of flights, taxis and hotel accommodation.

At this point I was completing a MSc in Project and Program Management with my research paper being on Mental Health in the Project Environment, how apt was that as I was becoming a prime specimen to monitor and observe.

The train once again left the station but had more emergency stops along the way. Firstly for a lung infection in March, a bite received whilst on vacation in South Africa in May by a jumping spider which had caused my arm to swell and finally in July, an infection in my gut that saw me hospitalised once again for 7 days. At this point I was beginning to think that life would never be what it was pre infection, post biopsy, and this was the new norm of my life. During all this time from January to July, I was also undergoing many scans and tests as my consultant was now convinced I had indeed got cancer and that it was serious.

My life is but a shadow set across the footprint of my being and like my shadow will disappear into the setting sun with no trace of my existence unless you whisper my name into the wind of change to carry me forward into the memory of the generations to come after.

CHAPTER 6
NO HOPE

It was now July 2017 a full twelve months had passed since that innocuous phone call from my family doctor. Once again I found myself sitting on a bed awaiting biopsies to be taken. However, this time things were so different. It was a small room with two medical professionals in the room looking after me. Strange as it may sound but the fact that the room was small somehow put me at ease. The instructions followed about lie up on the bed. Bring your knees into your chest and try relax and take slow breaths. This time there were only five clicks as that was all the samples they required.

A few weeks prior to this I had undergone an MRI scan which had shown "something" unusual in my prostate. I recall getting the scan, here I was once again wearing the hospital gown lying on a bed as machines rotated around me at a speed. A plate was placed upon my stomach prior to commencing the scan, not that it was heavy but to me it felt like a lead anchor fixing me to the table. I found myself unable to control my breathing. 'What is going on with you Raymond', I kept saying to myself. In hindsight, I think I was encountering something of a panic attack. I knew within my very being that things were not going to turn out for the better, I knew I HAD cancer. No doctor or consultant had uttered these words to me but within my own mind I knew I had. Let's simply call say a doctor called intuition visited me that day.

> Raymond we have taken the biopsies now, if you feel alright I want you to slowly straighten yourself up and place your feet on the floor. In your own good time stand up and the nurse will help you outside, we just need you to sit there for a few minutes before going back up to Urology Department.

I sat alone in a brightly lit corridor, I could hear machines working and random medical staff walked by, always politely smiling in my direction, did they know, can they tell by looking at my face I have cancer. These were the questions momentarily going on inside my mind. Then a gentleman sat next to me. We introduced ourselves and he looked extremely worried. As we chatted he told me how a neighbour of his had called over previous night and explained what was going to happen but unintentionally I am sure ended up scaring this poor man. I reassured him, yes me, reassuring someone. It will be all fine, it is not painful, just an unusual sensation and will be over in less than 5 minutes. He was called and our conversation ended, I gave him a knowingly smile and nod as if to say you will be fine, trust me it will be okay.

I made my way back to the Urology department where I was asked to drink plenty of water as I would need to pass urine before they could discharge me. Not one for drinking copious amounts of water I duly followed the instructions and drank more water in that period of time than I would in a day but no luck as no urge to go to the toilet. The nurse came and sat beside Selena and I. She suggested that perhaps we should go for a walk around the hospital and even go have something to eat in the restaurant and drink more water. I was probably anxious after my last experience and that was causing me not being able to urinate. Funny now as I write this with the irony being I can't stop urinating now but such is life.

Off we went for a walk, hand in hand. These were the hands who had comforted me since I was a young boy, the hands who made me feel safe and loved. Selena had been by my side since we met as young children, we were inseparable although many an attempt was made to do so our love was never going to let that happen. My life was in her hands and no safer pair of hands for them to be in. She understood me and knew me better than I knew myself, she was aware of what was happening inside my head as I placed the blinkers on it. Like a race horse I only wanted to focus on the race in front of me, I did not want to be distracted by the sideshows or what was behind. We walked around for a bit and then ended up in the restaurant.

Conversation was minimal on my behalf and we both knew what the outcome would be but neither of us would dare say the words. How could we, who truly wants to sit across a table from the love of their life and say I have cancer. No such thoughts were going to be entertained, we were focused we were determined no matter the outcome we will fight this as one as we had always done in every encounter we came across in our lives together.

We made our way back to urology and I dutifully performed as requested but there were a number of clots in my urine. I was asked to delay my departure for a couple of hours and to drink more water. More water! Do you people not realise I am the human version of a camel and do not need to drink so much but if that is what it takes more water I will drink. Finally, we got the colour correct and I was discharged with strict instructions that any rise in temperature, excessive blood in my urine and I was to come straight back to A&E, no hesitation.

The day of the test results arrived, I sat in the waiting room which I had now done on many occasions and as I did so once again I looked perplexed at the height of the door to the room. Why I thought to myself does a door have to be so large, it must easily be over ten feet tall. These are the thoughts that preoccupy me on many a day, questioning the obvious looking for reasons and explanations when there are none to be found. The radio was playing and as usual RTE Radio One was on, it was early morning so news was the predominant discussion but I made no attempt to listen to it. I was calm, well, as calm as one can be waiting for such results. Selena was not with me that morning as I was actually bringing my father in for an appointment to the same consultant and my appointment was scheduled for later that evening.

His secretary greeted me with her friendly warm smile and informed me that she had spoken with our consultant and he had agreed to give me the results while I was here rather than making me wait till later that evening. This was good news and bad news as Selena was not with me, how would I cope without her by my side?

The lead boots were firmly affixed to my feet as our name was called and we went into the consultant's room. Each step was indenting my life upon the concrete floor as if it was wet cement time lining my existence. My father's results and diagnosis was dealt with promptly and at that time there were no issues for him to concern himself about. I asked my dad would he mind waiting outside while I got my results as I didn't want him to hear it before Selena. I owed her that much.

The door closed behind my dad, now I was alone with my future sitting facing me with his usual smile and thoughtful glance. The news was as I had predicted. I had cancer. Why was I suddenly shrinking in size and the room getting bigger, I see his lips moving but he is talking very slowly and silently, what is happening to me, can anyone see me anymore, do I exist, am I now a statistic, a number to go on some chart and graph displayed and discussed at a conference?

As I left the room, we shook hands as we always did and now the big decisions had to be made, what form of therapy or procedure I wanted to choose. So many decisions so little time but yet there was time. I was the one who felt it was slipping through my hands like the melting snow numbing me to life with the inner pain and turmoil.

I walked out of the reception room, glanced at my father, he knew, no words were said. Along the carpeted corridor we travelled, oh the memories of childhood were flooding back when I couldn't walk on carpet in stores as I had sensory overload. Now in the stillness and quietness of this corridor I was and always will be that child. Where was my mother now, why was she taken from me doesn't the universe know I NEED her right this moment. I want her tender caress. The kiss on the forehead as she slowly brushes away my fringe, her scent, her ability to ease the noise and pain of this cruel harsh world. Oh mum, you are missed every day and some more than others, they stole you from me years before your last breath through dementia but we still smiled, giggled and laughed. Your presence will be felt tonight when the darkness tucks all into bed, you will slip into my room, lift me up in your arms and rock me to sleep, humming me an endless tune of affection, love and compassion.

I took out my phone, looked at it and went to dial the only phone number that needed to be phoned at this point, Selena. She answered immediately, I couldn't say the word. I fumbled and was incoherent fighting back my tears so as not to frighten her. We were both silent, our breaths were doing the talking of our voices, I needed to get home to the safety of her embrace. It was a silent journey in the car with my dad as I dropped him off at his house, the good byes were brief, and he knew I needed to be elsewhere. No thought was given by me as to how this must be impacting on him, his son diagnosed with an aggressive form of prostate cancer at age 55. How could this be happening?

We had travelled a similar journey some ten years ago when I was picking him up from a consultant's appointment and he had been diagnosed with colon cancer. Now it was his turn to be the spectator and mine to be the patient. But we had fought tougher more prolonged battles than this together and we will not stand down to this one, not now, we will overcome whatever it is they throw at us.

Once again, Selena was waiting at the door, we embraced, hugged and tears silently ran down our cheeks merging into one just like we had on so many occasions. The numbness was quick to set in, the stealth at which our life was encapsulated by the surreal was quick. We were lost deep within a fog unable to find our way, the path was blurred and the hopelessness of situation was disarming our rational minds.

Silence was our coping mechanism as we simply sat and embraced. Who to tell next and in what order, oh why do we have to think of order at a time like this but we must phone the girls, our daughters.

What can I say here about our two girls? They are simply two of the most beautiful souls that ever walked this planet. Each different, unique and self-assured. They will have their own journey to travel on this path as I was only too aware from watching my father go through his journey. But as a family unit we were solid, cancer was going to have a battle on its hands, we were not sitting down and allowing this to dictate to us what life would be like for us.

Weeks passed and the numbness lingered for Selena and I always present always intruding. The time had come to discuss the options and the impact of each upon our life. There were a number of them that were just not applicable to our situation. Mine needed surgery and possible treatment alongside that. We visited with the necessary consultants and had information overload.

We were told I would need an operation, radiotherapy along with hormone treatment that would last approximately 3 years. The situation was grim but the spirit was rekindling and a spark was igniting deep down within us. Thankfully, we had an amazing consultant who would break everything down into meaningful manageable pieces and kept us focussed blocking out all the noises and distractions.

Finally a decision was made, we would go for radical prostatectomy using robotic surgery. No further decision would be made about any treatment till after surgery, even though the radiotherapist was anxious to get me on hormone treatment immediately. As our consultant said, we are on a long journey and need to jump the first fence before we even anticipate about the possible other fences that will be encountered.

On the day of surgery we were upbeat, finally we were going in to remove this cancer. We smiled and joked while I was being prepped. The time came for the nurse to wheel my bed to theatre, Selena and I embraced one last time and kissed. This was it. we were on our way to the next adventure in our life together, we had fought so many battles before this was not going to get the better of us. My hand slowly slipped from her grasp and as I looked back at her I immersed myself in the beauty that stood before me. This girl chose me at fifteen and here now forty one years later she was still standing by my side protecting me from my own demons.

I was brought to a small room where the medics explained that I would be placed in a sand bed so that no movement would take place during my operation. They explained how the bed would be tilted slightly with my head lower and the surgeon would be sitting behind my head operating the robotic instruments. I was in the theatre for approximately six hours and am glad to say I have no recollection of anything other than the needle being placed into my arm, counting to three and then sheer darkness ensued.

The next recollection I have is someone saying, 'Raymond you are back in recovery all is good'. I went in and out of sleep all night but one memory and sensation was that of having pain in my bladder as if I needed to go to the toilet but I had a bag on me so my bladder was emptying automatically.

I woke the next morning to find a bag coming out of my side draining my wound and a numbness down below. Before I had time to gather my thoughts a lovely lady entered my room, she enquired how I was and informed me that she was a nurse's help and was here to aid me when I showered. My initial thought was, 'hold on a second let me wallow in my own self-pity here I have just had radical surgery and my life is going to change irreversibly from this point on'. But her gentle determination and soothing smile gave me no other option than to surrender to her demands. She was right too, I felt so much better after the shower and she was discreet and gentle in the manner she conducted it. For the first time in a long time I was beginning to feel human again as unawares to myself the cancer had been slowly draining me, sucking me of energy and life like a vampire bleeding their victim for their own self existence lurking in the darkness of wellbeing.

I lay in my hospital bed wearing the gown I had surgery in contemplating why I was feeling the way I was. Yes, I know I had just had surgery but there was something else trying to rise up inside of me. The senior urology nurse came to visit me that morning and we discussed the operation, how it was a success and how pleased the surgeon was with the way things went.

Suddenly, I found myself talking to her about the child abuse I had suffered. Initially, she was surprised at my candid outspoken nature about this topic but was happy to see I was willing to talk so openly about it. I did not realise at that point that she was the first person outside of my family that I had discussed this with so openly. It was as if the removal of the cancer had given me permission to release the shackles of self-guilt, the oppression that had weighed so heavily upon me and to release myself from the grips of its claw like hands dragging me into the darkness where humiliation laid silently awaiting my arrival.

Prior to this I may have indicated the abuse but to open up so freely was new and it felt good. There and then I decided that society was no longer holding me prisoner to the guilt of another who preyed upon my innocence and stole my inner child vanquishing him to the torture chambers of self-worth. That day was the beginning of a new journey, a reunion between my younger self and I. it was time to acknowledge who he was, it was time to take his hand in mine, to feel the purity and innocence that existed in him. He had silently and diligently kept his secret, he had been banished from society, never to be allowed express his feelings. It was time and I now had to seek his forgiveness so he could rest at peace.

Cast your net across the ocean that is your life so that when the famine of loneliness sets in you have an abundance of memories to feed upon until the next excursion on the open seas of life.

CHAPTER 7
HOPE RESTORED

The surgeon was extremely happy with my progress and two days after surgery I was discharged, sent packing with my bag strapped to my leg and instructions on how to empty and change it at night. Selena performed the role of nurse, carer and counsellor for the coming period. I was glad to get home and be once again in my own bed, I had not been absent for long from it but it was my safe place.

At the outset of this journey I had made a promise to myself and it was to allow myself be vulnerable and share my fears with Selena. I knew the journey was going to be a tough one and hiding my feelings would only exacerbate my illness and prolong the recovery period. Obviously, this is easier said than done if you are someone who doesn't normally expose their inner fears. It was not because Selena and I would never talk openly but more that I had become a master at suppressing my own anxieties not just to others but more importantly to myself. I now had to teach myself to be open and expose myself, be prepared to lay bare the open wounds that had been covered in a band aid of self-survival for decades. Removing this plaster was going to hurt.

It was a non-typical morning for me when the decades of self-preservation came crumbling down upon my head as the avalanche of my anxieties, fears and darkness shrouded across my body like a death shroud. I had managed for decades to hide my inner child locked away in a box lowered to the depths of the dark murky seabed of self-depravity. Lying in isolation as the darkness became deeper and the essence of hope evaporated to the surface never to look back in favour to apologise but rather only to seek out the future.

To suddenly peel back the layers would be like peeling back the skin that covered your veins exposing them to the daylight but rather being charged with electricity, touching them would surely mean immediately shortcutting the main fuse board and tripping the switch. Anyone who would come near would only end up receiving a sharp shock to their body too.

But now here I laid, exposed to the environment around me, suffering in pain and bathing in exhaustion, how could I have let myself be this vulnerable, where was my self-worth. I am not usually the type who crumbles into their pillow but this was me right now. I could no longer hold in the despair, the anxieties and the oppression that had laid dormant. My bowel had failed to work, I was in agonising pain, and the reality of my situation was now firmly looking back at me, staring me down in the face eyeball to eyeball with no disguise to hide behind. I looked into Selena's eyes, reached across the bed to her and for the first time I can ever recall cried uncontrollably in her arms as she soothed my pains away.

She had been expecting it knowing the signs I had ignored for so long, my seven year old self was now been cradled, hugged and comforted the way he had been seeking for almost fifty years. He had laid diligently dormant never dare exposing his feelings always being the good little boy and falling into line. Keeping the secret like he had been told to do, but here he was now exposed to the light of the morning for the first time in so long, he had raised up from the depths of the murky waters of self-sacrifice to save me. He knew I needed him now more than ever before, never flitching or taken a second glance he knew his time had come to save me rather than I save him. He was magnanimous in his comfort whereas I should have been seeking his forgiveness. It is so difficult for anyone who has not been abused to truly understand the affect and impact it has on one's life. We spend a lifetime hiding the shame as if that shame was ours to bear when, in fact, there is no shame that should be placed upon us. We feel guilty for what we did as if we were a willing participant but there is no guilt that should be born upon us. We are the innocent shameless party here and the perpetrator is the one who walks free never glancing back at the path of destruction they have laid upon our life's journey.

That day was the worst day of my journey from a mental health perspective but many more challenges laid ahead of me. The morning I was to get the bag removed was the day of storm Ophelia and the media was stating that we all must stay at home and only venture out if in cases of emergency. Selena looked at me and knew immediately there was no point in asking me whether we should postpone the appointment. I was heading straight in to the Beacon hospital and getting this bag removed. We drove from our home in Blessington across the mountains and over by the M50 motorway where it felt like we were driving across the city after an Armageddon event as no traffic was on the roads.

I walked down that long corridor on the fifth floor as if I was heading to an awards ceremony, I just wanted the bag removed as it had become another milestone in my head that had to be met on the road to recovery. We were ushered into a room where the nurse explained how the procedure would take place and that immediately after removing the bag I may have leakage, particularly when I stood up. All I could hear in my head was myself shouting take the bloody thing off me now!

One deep breath and the tube was out, no pain or discomfort. I was once again set free to walk with no tube dangling between my legs and bag attached to my ankle, this is what it must have felt like to get the shackles removed from your ankles when a prisoner all those decades ago. The moment of truth patiently waited for my momentous vertical upright position. This could only be akin to taking the first steps on the moon as I turned around on the bed, sat up and then that moment when the world media should have been televising me live as I placed my feet to the ground, one small step for man one giant step for prostateless men. The sole of my shoe gently found the floor, I gradually straighten my back up and then I was vertical and the flood gates opened like a bouncing bomb breaching a dam. No leakage but rather a flood of biblical proportion descended inside my pants. Yep I had been given a pad but what I needed was a nappy, strike that, what I needed was a reservoir!

This was the beginning of the journey that would hit me mentally more than physically. I was innocent to the journey of passage that laid ahead. Statistically on paper there was no concerns to be anxious about, the odds were good to getting a full recovery including control over my bladder. As for Erectile Dysfunction that was to be a permanent feature of my life, no, our life. This was/is a journey that if you are in a relationship a couple take together not dissimilar to the impact either breast or cervical cancer would have on a relationship. The similarities are stark and the impact immense on one's relationship. You now have to redefine what that relationship means to both of you as it cannot be purely based on sexual appetite, but rather on something far more tangible and sustaining.

We often hear from women about the emotional turmoil that ensues mastectomy but rarely do we hear about men's struggles following a procedure that may leave them permanently suffering from erectile dysfunction. Then add into that mix permanent leakage should the incontinence issue not resolve itself. Now you not only feel inadequate from a relationship perspective but you are left wearing pads 24/7 every day of the year. Your life can become void of spontaneity if you allow it to take control of you.

I recall being on the national airwaves doing an interview in my attempt to raise awareness around prostate cancer. It was Newstalk and the interviewer was Ivan Yates. I had deliberately targeted Ivan to conduct an interview with me because at the time I felt he was one of very few radio broadcasters who would not be afraid to ask the difficult questions. He openly admitted that if it was him he was not so certain that he would be announcing to the world what I was opening up about. But to me that was the very issue, men were going underground about this illness and the potential side effects.

I say potential because not every man will end up with permanent erectile dysfunction and/or incontinence. In fact, it is rare to have either and more rare to have both permanently after such a procedure but yet no one was talking about it. We were becoming the silent sufferers in a society that at the same time was talking about everything and anything, even photographing their meals and posting them on social media. But yet the more serious and life impacting issues were being I guess photoshopped out of our lives.

I have appeared on national radio shows and indeed in more recent times in the printed media talking about prostate cancer. I was used to being interviewed at this stage because of my job and I have a ritual that I never listen back to any interview I do. Because when I am being interviewed I state what my mind is thinking at that point in time so I do not want to revisit it. Tomorrow I might feel differently and explain the same issue in a totally different manner.

Ivan was the true gent that he doesn't want any of his listeners to know he is. When I came out of the studio one of his researchers came over to me who was listening in to the interview to thank me for being so bluntly honest and open. In fact, this same situation has happened on a number of occasions by different journalists who thank me for my frankness and openness. But to me I don't see the issue, events have happened in my life, they were not ones I had planned or indeed wanted but they happened. I now have to deal with that and find the best way of coping with where I find myself.

I arrived home from the radio studio and once again I was emotionally drained from the meeting. The interview was to be aired in a week and we were duly notified of the date and time. My wife and daughter listened in. As for me, I retreated to my desk, placed my earphones on and blasted the music through my body. It was as if I was providing self-induced radiotherapy to eradicate the cancer of the past, the memories of the abuse, and everything that happened to me. I had never and still don't think my life is any greater a challenge than anyone else's. Neither do I think my life is a bad one as there are so many people out there suffering far more trauma in their day to day existence than I have ever had.

After the show had ended the verdict was in on the interview and from a totally bias standpoint both my wife and daughter felt I had done good, no red X's there so and I can now proceed to the next stage of the competition, Raymond's Got Talent (RGT).

The following day an email came into my company mailbox from someone who had listened to the interview and felt I was very negative about the entire process. They said they too had a prostatectomy and thankfully for them they had recovered fairly unscathed with bladder control and no erectile dysfunction. I was happy for them but somewhat perturbed that they wished to silence me as I would be frightening off men from getting checked. If anything, that was the furthest thing from my mind. I was and am trying to encourage men to get checked so they don't have to go through what I went through.

To me this is the issue, men are in general silenced when they try to open up. I recall the time my wife miscarried our baby. The devastation of that experience was huge and many of her friends called to the house to see her. The memory has stayed with us forever. She had been feeling unwell and we went to our family doctor. He said it was likely she was losing the baby. I immediately suggested we go visit the obstetrician who had delivered our other two daughters but the doctor said it was unlikely we would get an appointment that quick. Not one to be told what to do I phoned the consultant. His secretary took my message and within an hour he was on the phone to Selena. She explained the situation and he told her to get straight over to him.

We arrived at the Rotunda maternity hospital, ushered quickly to his rooms and he took full control, Selena would have to be brought in and stay overnight. I felt totally useless, inadequate and surplus to requirements. I was of no value and the medics were taking care of Selena. Whilst they did so I was left waiting outside, gazing aimlessly out the window, staring at nothing and wondering why. Then out of nowhere flew a white butterfly, fluttering its delicate tissue like wings outside the sash window. There was a gap and it flew into the room, circled around me and landed in front of me. At this precise moment Selena was being treated and our baby departing this world that they were far too delicate and precious for. To this day butterflies have a very special place in our hearts. When we returned home grief set in. How does one mourn a baby they never knew or saw but yet their absence was real. We would never have candles to blow out on their birthday cake, we would never place their tiny hands in ours, and we could never kiss their perfect little toes. Gone, never to be seen.

My brother-in-law and his wife came to visit us soon after and as usual through instinct they comforted Selena first but then for the first time since we lost our baby someone acknowledged I had lost a child too. It was my sister-in-law, she quietly came over to me in the room and simply asked how I was doing. A simple gesture but one that made my grief feel real too. It is so easy to side-track the father of the miscarried child but their loss is genuine, they need to acknowledge they were an expectant parent too. There are no visible signs for all to see but deep down inside of them they are aching, feeling the absence of a life they so wanted but has now departed.

The issue here is that because of the way society has been moulded to think of the male species being all strong and void of emotional requirements we can tend to be overlooked at traumatic times throughout our lives. I am not saying that we should breakdown and cry every time we break a nail or cut ourselves shaving but there needs to be a better understanding of the emotional needs of men. There needs to be an environment in which they are comfortable talking about issues that are impacting on their lives without feeling they are weak or a lesser person for doing so. At the same time whether male or female we have to realise that life is tough, it is not an environment in which we are surrounded in cotton wool and nothing bad will ever happen to us. We have to be able to survive rejection, failure, and loss.

Life should not be seen through a photo shopped soft lenses where the imperfections of our lives are erased. We need to learn to celebrate our imperfections and uniqueness. We need to be able to withstand the storms that will undoubtedly visit upon our lives from time to time. In my opinion, rejection is not a reflection upon you but rather on the person who rejected you. We do not need to morph ourselves into someone else's image of who they think we should become but rather if they truly want to be part of our lives then they must accept us for who we are.

I wrote the poem White Noise as a reflection upon how in today's world we seem to be more interested in social media traction than human interaction. And yet when we hit a crisis or turbulent period in our lives it is important to have interaction with real friends rather than just virtual ones. That is not to say you cannot make close friends from social media but rather you need to realise what is real and what is cosmetically camouflaged to appear real.

White Noise

The never ending white noise of this world is filling the voids within the crevices of our being that once resided for humanity, we have capitulated our social responsibility in favour of social media.

Where 'Likes' are more important than empathy and virtual friends are collected like collector cards in favour of lasting friendships.

Longevity is measured in terms of social media traction rather than endurance throughout time. The world is closing in, becoming smaller but yet we have never been so far apart.

Communication is happening all round us but no one is talking, no one is present in the moment actively engaging with you. We are in danger of overcrowded isolation in this life form.

Our thoughts are locked deep within, never allowed to see the light of day, as to do so may impact on our following. We rather only show our true selves through filter and touch-ups but never bare naked our soul.

The positivity bunny rabbits are bouncing all around, quick to launch in with their never ending enthusiasm and positive slogan without contemplating your need, anxieties and suffering. Everything can be cured with a Meme and evangelistic quote.

Weakness is not tolerated in this world of soft filters and touch-ups. Your suffering is their memento as they collect the injured souls like reward stamps to promote their self-importance.

Where to find solitude in this white noise of life, how to switch the noise off to find inner contentment without the need of notification alerts.

To go back to basics, but what are basics. I need my soul to heal, I need my mind to be at peace, I need my eyes to close and relax.

Like the faceless victims of Hiroshima all that

remains is the dark outline were my life once paused

to take a momentary breath in this life

CHAPTER 8
THE GOOD, BAD AND UGLY

Cancer is a dreadful disease but I can honestly say that I have never had so many positives in my life happen since I was diagnosed. The good is that I have learnt more about myself in these past two years than ever before, I have found strengths I never knew existed but also I have allowed myself to be vulnerable and in doing so have found strength in that too. I have made friends that I would otherwise have never encountered, fellow Prostate Cancer warriors in particular a band of brothers whom I have named The Four Tenas. If you are not familiar with men's incontinence pads made by Tena this may have gone over your head. We are self-deprecating and take no prisoners when it comes to talking about our illness, we range from mid-forties to mid-fifties and come from different backgrounds.

The comfort I have personally found by interacting with the Four Tenas is immeasurable. We are truly a band of brothers jointly fighting our way through a battle royal that rages on inside our bodies but more importantly in our heads. The ability to be able to discuss our most inner fears whilst at the same time injecting humour has been a huge help to all. We find strength from one another and we support each other when we fall because fall we will.

Each of us has a different life journey to talk about but yet it is the same, in a similar fashion to someone reading this who may never get prostate cancer or indeed any form of cancer but will have a journey that will have many similarities to ours. The people I have met have been all inspiring, women fighting for care for their ill children, others surviving their own journey with cancer or escaping from abusive relationships.

I would encourage anyone who is on a journey to seek out friends that can assist them through their ordeal, true friendship can never be underestimated and may be found in the strangest of places. For us four it was through Twitter as we all were tweeting about Prostate Cancer. The power of talking is immense but can only work when active listening is also taking place and if for whatever reason you find it too difficult to talk about your deepest inner concerns then I suggest you write them down in a journal and get them out from within. To do so will help release inner pressure and contribute to the healing process.

As mentioned at the outset of this book I am no medic and have no qualifications in relation to mental health etc. but I am someone who has been on and is still on a journey, one that impacts me physically and indeed mentally. I have my own coping mechanism and am extremely fortunate with having a loving, caring and understanding partner by my side. I also have the support of family and friends. I hope you too can find your support mechanism and support group.

The bad part of cancer is the impact it can have on your life until such time that you manage to find your coping mechanism for dealing with it. However, even when you do find that there will be days that it all just becomes too much. The important thing is that on those days don't be hard on yourself. Allow yourself the space to be vulnerable and even self-pitying as there is no shame in showing weakness. But don't linger there too long, find the positives in life once again and have those all-important friends around you who are your support group.

For me the bad side effects of prostate cancer are the incontinence and erectile dysfunction. To still have to wear incontinence pads 24/7 two years after surgery can on the days that are slowly becoming more rare wreck my head. Simple things like going out to town, car journeys greater than an hour or on holidays are all planned in more detail as I calculate how long the journey time is, where and when am I likely to be able to take a toilet break. Remembering to bring spare pads and indeed clothes if I am going to be gone for long periods just in case of the rare accident that I may need to change.

I often joke to myself that I am going to start a Prostate Cancer Guide to the best toilets across Europe so my fellow warriors can locate clean toilets if and when required. In the early days of my journey with the cancer when I was wearing the nappies I recall having to explain to my eldest grandson what was happening with me as he was worried about me. The two of us went for a little walk, he was ten at the time. I explained how Pappy had an operation, it was for a form of cancer men get and that the doctors are confident they removed it all. Of course Joshua being who he is wanted to dig deeper into the illness so we talked about how one of the issues I was having was that I found it difficult to control my bladder. I simply said that it was like his younger sister who had to wear nappies and so did he and indeed everyone when they were a baby. Over time we developed our muscles that helped us control our bladder. My muscles that control my bladder had to be developed once again and that is why I had to wear nappies. He was content with that explanation and now two years on he is happy that I am able to lift him and his sisters for hugs. He knows I still have issues but he also knows that is ok. In some ways it is a good lesson for him to know that when we encounter challenges in life we can overcome them and indeed his two sisters are also aware of this.

The ugly part of prostate cancer is without doubt the mental challenges it places on you. Having spoken to not just the Four Tenas about this but now we are almost a choir as more and more men join our WhatsApp group the one thing we all have in common is the mental challenge. However, that said the ability to unload in a safe environment with fellow sufferers is a huge benefit. I recall during the early weeks post-surgery talking to a friend and explaining how I would wake up in the morning, and the pain I felt along with discomfort was bad. I would slowly get out of bed and make my way to the bathroom but by the time I would reach the toilet my bladder would have emptied into the nappy. Over the days which then turned into weeks this played heavily on my mind and it was like a drip of water slowly dropping down onto a surface eroding away its exterior hard protective cover. I would then return to my bed and fall back asleep for about an hour, that period of time was my utopia, I would be relaxed, in no pain and always slept soundly. Then when I got up and dressed I would make my way downstairs for breakfast but before going to the kitchen I would descend the stairs holding my nappy disposable sack. Open the hall door to go outside and walk to the bin. This was my walk of shame. This is not to say that anyone made me feel shameful or indeed I had anything to be ashamed of but rather it was that moment that simply reinforced my life had now changed irreversibly and I had to come to terms with that. I am happy to report that I did come to terms with it and now there is no walk of shame but rather simply a walk to the bin to discard some rubbish.

Erectile Dysfunction (ED) is another aspect of this disease that at times leaves you feeling like an empty vessel. You have been stolen of those intimate moments with your partner and the journey can be a tough one for some. It can creep up on you when you least expect it, that is to say there are moments when the enormity of your situation is too heavy a load to carry. You lie in bed with your partner and there can be a sense of feeling inadequate, no longer able to contribute to the relationship like you had before and this can gnaw at your mental health. This is not something that everyone who has prostate cancer will suffer from but that does not mean we should exclude it from the book. My aim with this book was to 'keep it real', my experiences of which I am the only one who can talk truthfully about them. There are devices and intervention that may help like pumps or injections into the penis. However, each person is an individual and they will have to make that decision as to whether or not they are for them.

The Absent Lover is a poem I wrote to Selena approximately 18 months after my surgery. It's about the conflict that raged in my head over being absent in our bed even though I was physically lying beside her. I understand from talking with women who have experienced either breast or cervical cancer they have similar feelings. It is the unspoken side effect of these cancers that impact on our physical relationship more from our mental health perspective. That is not to say that every person who has any of these cancers will struggle with this but rather that some may.

The Absent Lover

I am present but yet I am absent, my physical being lies here but my inner soul has vacated this emotionally constipated vessel

I long to hold you close but now find I have built an invisible barrier, the barbed wire of my own deprived emotions is preventing the tender touch, the closeness, the emotional warmness and tenderness of your caress

I crawl into bed at night contemplating my existence, my journey and feel void of all emotion, overwhelmed by the never ending noise within, the voices, the images, the silent screams

What lies ahead for us, where do we go now, how do we reignite that special love we have for each other, when will this all end, how can we survive this intrusion, this mistress that has entered our relationship, the unwanted third party?

I am coping but yet I am not, I've neglected you for the sake of gathering my own sanity but to what price, we speak, you listen, you comfort me, but I am on the outside just observing, when will I be present again?

So many questions and so few answers, kind words, glances, nods of acknowledgements, texts, messages, they don't replace the emptiness I feel, the abandonment of my life, the war raging inside, the battles are easily won but the war is harder to overcome

Writing is the easiest bit, the words flow, the letters dance amongst the sheets and collide into a meaningful sentence but they are oh so hard to say aloud, to admit to oneself how you truly feel, to hear those words aloud, that's the torture deep down within

How dare the world continue, does it not realise the suffering contained within, does it not hear the silent deep throated squeals for help, the utter deprivation of humanity as we suffer with dry tears streaming down our faces, so many suffering so few listening

Ah to listen, that is the thing, the art, to keeps one's mouth shut and stay within the moment, the conversation, but its oh so hard to listen, so much easier to speak and fill the silent void of incompatible sympathetic nonsense

This life, this debt we must pay to the paymaster for something we never sought. Who are they to say who should suffer, the so called all caring loving vapours of influential tormenters, who gave them the right to righteousness, who are they to say what sin is and when life should end?

Close the door, leave the noise outside, breathe slowly and release the angst of the inner turmoil, I shall return one day, be present once more in your life, be present once more in your bed, be the person you fell in love with, be the partner you deserve, but for now I am the absent lover.

If I am not true to myself why then should others be true to me. If I have no self-respect how then can I respect others? If I do not cherish life how then can I experience it? If I am always a victim and never a survivor who then truly wins. I live to love and love to live in tandem we will fall.

CHAPTER 9
MENTAL HEALTH

'Nothing's so bad that it couldn't be worse,' the words my dad has said so many times in relation to his own journey with colon cancer and now he was saying it to me about my close encounter with it. What a strong statement, for every aspect of your life whether in business or personal life. No matter how bad you think it is now it could always be worse so let that thought lighten your load, feel confident in the fact that no matter how hard things may seem right now someone else is experiencing something far worse. Life is not an easy journey and I believe it is not meant to be. In a world where we want to shelter our children from every aspect that they may find challenging is perhaps not the correct course. We need to have the small knocks so we build up a resilience in order to help us through when we have the hard knocks.

My life has had many knocks and I am not advocating that everyone should have similar challenges in their lives but what I am advocating is that we need to be allowed to fall and hurt ourselves. By doing so, we will learn to get back up and be stronger for those knocks that we have encountered. Ask yourself if successful sports people had won every single tournament they entered how it would impact upon them when one day they lose that all important match. There is a growing unconscious bias developing whereby we want to see every child rewarded for every sports game, challenge and competition they enter. But is that truly building character and resilience within them? What about the children who came first, second and third should their effort not be exclusively rewarded?

Statistics are now telling us that in the future one out of every two people will encounter cancer at some stage in their lives. How are they going to cope with that if it becomes the first true challenge they have met. By all means shelter our children so they have a safe, loving and caring environment but teach them how to lose magnanimously too. Let them know failure is not a negative that from those failings success will eventually come, the key to any success is determination and self-drive with the ability to withstand the knocks and tribulations that will undoubtedly be experienced along the way.

Mental health is something that affects every single person in this world whether it be their personal challenge or their loved ones. At some stage in our lives we will cross the abyss of this health issue and it is something that we need to be prepared to acknowledge and recognise. We must see strength in our weakness and understand that it is perfectly okay to feel overwhelmed, insecure and lost at times. The death of a love one, severe illness or even loss of a job can have a devastating effect on an individual's wellbeing.

It could be we fear that it may impact our career, we have a preconceived concept that it is a sign of weakness and to openly admit it would have a devastating impact on our professional and personal lives. We all know the slogan, 'it's OK not to be OK' but do we truly prescribe to that belief or are we simply providing lip service to it. And what happens when someone opens up to you and says, 'I'm not OK.' Then what? Can you honestly say you would know how to handle that?

Men, in particular, try their hardest to close down the conversation by saying something like, 'sure we all have problems, it will be grand, let's go for a drink and that will cheer you up.' But what that person really needs is for you to stay quiet and just listen, be present with them and in the moment. Show them compassion and comfort. Provide a safe environment for them to open up. They may wish to talk about something that is impacting their health, a loss they are experiencing (even a breakdown in their relationship is a grieving experience) the main thing is you know how to behave when they say those things to you.

Of course, we will all encounter the homosapien dinosaur male who will brush this off and say 'get a grip will you, don't start acting like a hormonal female you're better than that.' But they too will one day breakdown and cry, when they get cut they too bleed like us all, they have fears, anxieties and demons they don't want to surface.

Mental health is without doubt getting a growing awareness right across the world. Society is seeing the negative impact it has by ignoring its existence. We only have to look at the suicide rates where every minute of every day a man commits suicide somewhere in the world. In Ireland, eighty percent of all suicides are male and most common age is mid-twenties to mid-thirties. Suicide can be glamorised amongst our younger generation where there is a sense of notoriety associated with it by the attention perhaps provided in the media etc.

I was speaking with one of my fellow prostateless buddies and he explained to me how an ex-partner of his was so overwhelmed with the mental issues caused by prostate cancer and the impact it had on his personal life. The individual was unable to resume normal life, wouldn't go outside the house and eventually suicided. As a heterosexual male, I was totally unaware of the impact within the gay community that prostate cancer had. I am extremely glad of my friend's candid and open approach to explain to me his journey and the impact that it is having on his physical, personal and mental health. There is no doubt that our paths would never have crossed but for this illness, at some level I am grateful that we have met and indeed feel that I now have a lifelong friend.

Since contacting cancer I can honestly say that my life is no longer the same, it has been enriched so much by the people I have met, friendships that have been formed and just comradery from my fellow prostate cancer champions. I never expected to have positives from this illness but I have and have to admit that my life is richer by those who have now entered it.

And it is not just men but women too, suddenly I find myself interacting with so many more people on Twitter who have had a similar journey whether that be from cancer, being in an abusive relationship, challenges in life or just likeminded individuals.

This book is only being written because of my journey and that in itself has brought happiness to me. I have had many personal messages from people who have either heard me on the radio, read an interview in a newspaper or followed me on social media letting me know how much my openness has helped them. My aim at the outset was to start a conversation even for just one individual and I now believe that many conversations have been started and will continue on from this. That makes me personally feel good and my journey justified in opening up publicly.

I often wonder who I would have been if all these episodes I have spoken about in this book had never happened to me.

What if I hadn't been born to such a caring, loving and understanding mother who was ahead of her time on parenting.

What if I hadn't been born dyslexic or with a mild autism streak running through me. Would I be like "normal" people living in a black and white world or worse still a grey one? Because of my uniqueness I live inside a rainbow, a world filled with colour. I am empathic to people's journeys, I feel their pain and understand their anxieties. I don't see things in the normal way but rather through a pin hole of a lens that is honed in providing a segmented view.

In my world, square pegs fit into round holes. Individualism is celebrated and standards are frowned upon. Yes I have my little idiosyncrasies like having to have the volume turned up to a number that is divisible by 5, requiring precision when punching holes in paper to be filed, needing tidiness in my workspace and at home. Clutter causes me distraction.

What if I had not been sexually abused as a child would I have developed my caring nature, would my sense of empathy exist, would I feel such a strong urge to do something about the suffering children around the world?

What if I had not been bullied, would my dark sense of humour developed, would I feel the pain of those who are trodden upon by others? Would I have been a bully?

What if my mother had not been so ill and inspiring? Would I still have the same values and zest for life that I do now? Would I be blind to death and the impermanence of life like so many are? Would I have realised we are all terminally ill? Would I have the inner strength to survive anything life throws at me? Would I have made friends with death at such a young age, knowing never to fear it but neither to hasten its arrival?

What if we had not experienced a miscarriage would I truly understand the fragility of life? Would I have taken the birth of my other two daughters for granted and how could I have empathised with my daughter when she had her miscarriage? How would I have been able to say, I know I do feel your pain, your loss and anger?

What if I had not been made redundant at such a young age? Would I have ever setup my own companies? Would I have taken the path I have and developed the skills I did?

What if my father had not got colon cancer would I have had the strength to fight my battle with the disease the way I did? Would I have known how to stare it down and come out the other side?

What if my mum had not got dementia would we have had those moments that we shared allowing me to be the nurturer and provide the hugs, cuddles and kisses?

What if my wife had not suffered with depression and had a nervous breakdown, would I be so patient with others, understanding and caring? Through her struggles I have gained strength from her weakness and inner strength. She is someone I can only aspire to become, she is caring, loving and, most of all, a true lady. I would undoubtedly have had a far more different life if our paths had not crossed when we were ten years old. If she had not agreed to be my girlfriend at age fifteen and have stayed by my side since. She is the cool breeze on a warm summer day that gently rolls over my skin. She is the warmth on a cold winter's night but more importantly she is the woman who chose me as her lifelong companion and who never fails to amaze me.

What if I had not contracted cancer would I have met all the inspiring people I have who are cancer survivors too like Vicky Phelan, John Wall, Jim Corcoran or Bill Kelly? Lifelong friends like Peter McVeigh and Karl Smyth would perhaps have not come into my life and if they had would not have stayed but rather passed on. Angelina McDonnell O'Neill and Paula Delaney are two other ladies who crossed my cyber doorstep and inspire me similar to Jessica Bowes, and Norah Casey. People like Gareth O'Callaghan who is on a huge journey himself but still takes time out to drop in from time to time to see if I am doing well.

I could go on as the list is endless, so many people have stopped whilst on their own journey and took the time out to bring me in from the cold for shelter. They wrapped me in their security blanket of hope, love and affection. They showed me that in a world of fragility and hurt that there is always a helping hand, a kind voice and most importantly a virtual hug when needed most. These are the unsung heroes of this world, the people who really matter.

I am content with my life and comfortable with whom I am. When you find yourself then this somewhat abstract world of confusion and distraction makes sense. You find your purpose and more importantly self-worth. My life path has been scattered with all inspiring and motivational people, none were what you would call famous they were just "ordinary" people who lived an average life. But each of them left a thread in the fabric of the cloth that shrouds around me.

When we walk by a house we know not what goes on behind those doors, whether it is a home of love and laughter or a house seeping with emotional turmoil. People come out of them and their deepest scars may never surface onto their face, their laughter can be cries of pain and their infectious good humour could be the camouflage of turmoil. So often we hear people say, 'I never knew they were in so much pain'. How often when we ask people how are they do we truly want them to answer that question? We need to take care of one another because one day we will want to be asked how we are doing.

Every single one of us have a personal journey to take and no one else can take that journey for us. We are going to fall down, we are going to get hurt and we are going to look in the mirror one day and perhaps not know who is staring back at us. We have to find inner strength as it won't come looking for us. We have to enjoy the small moments as they are the precious ones.

If and when you get down don't be too hard on yourself, allow yourself the space and freedom to indulge in that space for a short period. It is perfectly fine to feel overwhelmed at times, to feel like you just cannot cope anymore with the situation you find yourself in. Humans are the chameleons of social proprietary always blending into the situation they find themselves in. Rarely wanting to stand out from the crowd camouflaging themselves with conformity.

What if you never read this book or someone recited something from it? We learn from those around us, open your mind to what is about you, listen more than talk, observe more than posting the image, engage face to face more than conversing in cyber space. But most of all learn, observe and be present in the moment with you as you are the best teacher you will ever have.

What If..

What if I screamed my silent cries aloud would you think me mad?

What if I gave up would you think me sad?

What if I didn't exist would you miss me?

What if I asked for a hug would you think me needy?

What if I was just me would you still love me?

What if I never spoke of my fears would you think me brave?

What if I said how I truly feel would you listen?

What if I asked for forgiveness would you forgive me?

What if it had all never happened?

Our lives last no longer than the flutter of a butterflies wings when compared to the trees, make every moment count and never be afraid to utter the words, I love you as you might not get a second chance to do so…

INTERMISSION

My journey is not yet complete, will I complete everything I want to in life? Highly unlikely but will I enjoy attempting to do so, highly likely. As you have read my life has been peppered with many, I guess for want of a better word, challenges. But that is what life is about and we have to decide whether we will lie down under those challenges or rise to the occasion. I firmly believe that we all have it in us to overcome what life throws at us but we don't have to travel that path alone.

When I contracted prostate cancer the last thing that was on my mind was the sexual abuse I suffered as a young innocent boy. Have I dealt fully with that episode of my life? To be honest, I am not certain we ever come to a finality on such an episode. However, what I do think is that we learn how to cope with it, and the start of that journey is admitting to ourselves it happened. Then from there we decide how we want to take it forward whether that be through counselling or simply sharing the experience with a confidant that allows you the safe space to release those dark secrets that have laid dormant for so long.

My therapists are my dogs,; Mr Buttons and Miss Holly, they allow me the space to be vulnerable and they relax me by simply sitting by my side. My exorcism of those abusive events is found in writing, whether that be constructing a poem, writing a blog, book or simply tweeting about it. By releasing it from my inner thoughts into the written word is extremely helpful to me. I don't publicly publish everything I write, some are deleted but to actually hit the keyboards and watch the words evolve onto a page is therapeutic for me.

My challenges continue in life as I am finalising this book my father has been admitted to hospital. He contracted bladder and kidney cancer earlier this year and in July got his kidney removed. Unfortunately, that did not prevent the cancer moving to his hip. This is simply another challenge put in front of us that we will overcome regardless of what the outcome is. Always remember, life is impermanent and stay focussed on what is truly important to you.

I conclude this book with a poem I wrote on New Year's Eve 2017. I woke at approximately 07:00am and turned on my iPad, it had been just three months since my surgery and I was still at the stage of wearing full nappies. Selena laid asleep by my side, I looked at her resting peacefully. We had taken so many journeys on our life together and here we were once again sailing on the stormy waters navigating our destiny by the stars not really certain what was our final destination.

I contemplated many things that morning and asked lots of questions about life, its meaning, purpose and end game. I truly know not where this journey will take us, when it will end and if we will have accomplished what we set out to do at the beginning. However, what I am certain is that at the end of it she will still be lying by my side and we will overcome whatever is put in front of us. Also, I know that we will come out stronger from it all.

Finally, my parting message is for you all to remember that there is nothing so bad that it couldn't be worse!

New Year's Eve of Life

31 December 2017

I am not old but yet my body is slowing me down

Momentarily passing glances in the mirror show someone else

The person I knew myself to be is passed

My eyes deceive me as they look out from this vessel

The voices in my head sound familiarly youthful

I once shone brightly now I glisten

Like an ember from the fire of life

I shot forth shining brightly

Only to burn out and disappear into the darkness of death

My skin no longer fits me like a tight glove

Rather the tightness and elasticity has faded

Now my skin lies loosely upon the frame of my aching bones

As I sailed the waves on the sea of life

I find myself cast overboard being dragged to the depths of mediocrity

Shackled by the insignificance of my futile existence

Drowning in my self-pity I see the reflection of what could have been

The life that should have but for the distraction of self-indulgence

As I pass I no longer hear my name mentioned

Time will erase my futile existence from this life

Memories left behind will fade upon the passing of one generation

I lived for what, to do what, for whom

Am I truly alive or simply passing time to serve my Master, death?

Who am I to question the meaning of life?

Is there a meaning to life?

Is one life of greater or lesser importance than another's?

Is intelligence truly defined by academic ability?

Is empathy not more important than scholarly musings?

Has our surroundings and experiences defined what we've become

Where is the child within that was carefree?

The child that skipped as they walked

The child who was hungry for knowledge

The child who cried openly

The child who laughed loudly

The child who gave love unconditionally

Am I already dead if that child has left me?

Is my body simply an empty vessel of its former self?

Am I consuming time awaiting my final breath?

But yet I am not dead, I know not whether I am old

I know not the hour nor day of my demise

How then do I know if I am old?

What is old, an age, a concept, a state?

This life, this world, this hypocrisy we perform

We care for others only if they care for us

We rape the planet of its offerings to satisfy our self-indulgence

We kill one another in the name of different Gods but yet they are one

We see wealth as monetary gain rather than the ability to care for others

Homelessness is the status quo as politicians play with our lives

Refugees are not welcomed as we forget our history

Children die to provide us with our trinkets

The blind eye is everywhere as ignorance is our defence

My life will be short lived compared to the trees

But yet I feel I have lived long but to what avail

If I do not improve the life of others what difference is it how long I've lived?

Now as my life passes momentarily before me I see no value in its existence

Is it too late to change, do I want to change, why should I change

This life nay this existence is dragging me down

I'm consumed by the breadth of ignorance within and without

Does death have to mean my non-existence?

Rather I kill off that indulgent self and reborn myself from its embers

Like the Phoenix rises from the dirt to bring meaning back into life

Let me die this evening on the New Year's Eve of Life

Tomorrow I will emerge a better person

Death will be my saving grace as without it I cannot be reborn

I welcome you to my bed tonight to release the shackles

No longer will I drown in my own self indulgence

No longer will I exist for the mere sake of existence

Tomorrow will bring a new dawn to my life

One more chance to relieve my inner turmoil

One more chance to not fail my ideology

One more chance to breathe freely

Will you take this journey with me?

Or shall we die clutched in one another's arms

Sharing the breath of one another

Watching our eyes slowly fade

Feeling the grasp upon our bodies slip away

Till death do us part

Till the morning then

Till our hearts beat as one

Slowly, slowly, till stillness submits

End...

Raymond is a son, brother, husband, father and Pappy. He has lived a life of physical, emotional and mental challenges commencing from a young age when he was sexually abused right through to more recently when he commenced a journey with cancer. The purpose behind writing this book is to provide the catalyst to commence a conversation about the Emotionally Constipated (Irish) Male. Raymond feels many men bottle up their innermost fears and anxieties, but by having an open and healthy conversation about these issues we can provide a safe environment for us all to move forward. This book is written in the hope that it may just start that awkward conversation.

* Please feel free to follow me on Twitter @Aladinsane40

or email me at hello@raymondpoole.com

My website address is www.raymondpoole.com